Living Graciously on
Planet Earth

Living Graciously on
Planet Earth

Faith, Hope, and Love in Biblical,
Social, and Cosmic Context

Robert P. Vande Kappelle

WIPF *&* STOCK · Eugene, Oregon

LIVING GRACIOUSLY ON PLANET EARTH
Faith, Hope, and Love in Biblical, Social, and Cosmic Context

Copyright © 2016 Robert P. Vande Kappelle. All rights reserved. Except for brief quotations in critical publications or reviews, no part of this book may be reproduced in any manner without prior written permission from the publisher. Write: Permissions, Wipf and Stock Publishers, 199 W. 8th Ave., Suite 3, Eugene, OR 97401.

Wipf & Stock
An Imprint of Wipf and Stock Publishers
199 W. 8th Ave., Suite 3
Eugene, OR 97401

www.wipfandstock.com

PAPERBACK ISBN: 978-1-4982-9415-7
HARDCOVER ISBN: 978-1-4982-9417-1
EBOOK ISBN: 978-1-4982-9416-4

Manufactured in the U.S.A.   MAY 16, 2016

Unless otherwise noted, Bible quotations are from the *New Revised Standard Version of the Bible*, copyright © 1989 by the Division of Christian Education of the National Council of the Churches of Christ in the United States of America. Used by permission.

To Ryan Charles:
child of grace,
regal in demeanor and greatly loved

Hymn of Love

If I speak in the tongues of mortals and of angels, but do not have love, I am a noisy gong or a clanging cymbal. And if I have prophetic powers, and understand all mysteries and all knowledge, and if I have all faith, so as to remove mountains, but do not have love, I am nothing. If I give away all my possessions, and if I hand over my body so that I may boast, but do not have love, I gain nothing.

Love is patient; love is kind; love is not envious or boastful or arrogant or rude. It does not insist on its own way; it is not irritable or resentful; it does not rejoice in wrongdoing, but rejoices in the truth. It bears all things, believes all things, hopes all things, endures all things.

Love never ends. But as for prophecies, they will come to an end; as for tongues, they will cease; as for knowledge, it will come to an end. For we know only in part, and we prophesy only in part; but when the complete comes, the partial will come to an end. When I was a child, I spoke like a child, I thought like a child, I reasoned like a child; when I became an adult, I put an end to childish ways. For now we see in a mirror, dimly, but then we will see face to face. Now I know only in part; then I will know fully, even as I have been fully known. And now faith, hope, and love abide, these three; and the greatest of these is love.

—1 CORINTHIANS 13:1–13

Contents

Acknowledgments | ix

Introduction | 1
1. Cosmology, Anthropology, and Morality | 11
2. The Role of Religion | 23
3. The Promise of Nature | 34
4. The Promise of the World's Religions | 47
5. The Cardinal Virtues | 59
6. The Theological Virtues: Faith | 67
7. The Theological Virtues: Hope | 80
8. The Theological Virtues: Love | 93
9. Growing Graciously | 103
10. Epilogue: Realized Eschatology | 124

Appendix A Table of Interrelated Virtues | 133
Appendix B The Seven Virtues: A Brief Look | 134
Appendix C Love Never Fails: A Sermon | 136
Bibliography | 143
Subject/Name Index | 145

Acknowledgments

MORALITY IS OFTEN CONNECTED with spirituality, and rightly so. Every living world religion acknowledges a natural law, but such law is not the result of observation or of mere trial and error. Before there was a universe, there was a benevolent Spirit, graciously loving the emerging cosmos, instilling promise and bringing forth beauty. Ancient Jews and Christians viewed the natural world with awe, affirming it to be God's handiwork.

Because we humans are the product of divine promise, we are happiest when we bring beauty from ourselves and from others, and when we acknowledge and care for cosmic sacredness in its infinite manifestations. We do so best when we live virtuously, energized by faith, hope, and love, virtues so eternal and enduring that theologians have grouped them under the category of "theological" virtues.

The moral life is not to be lived dutifully or legalistically, but rather graciously, for without grace, all efforts at the moral life collapse. This I learned from Scripture, my parents, and from scholars such as Karen Armstrong, Marcus Borg, C. S. Lewis, Robin W. Lovin, and Huston Smith, master teachers and pioneers in the field of morality and spirituality.[1]

My gratitude extends to David Novitsky, Olga Solovieva, Dan Stinson, and Walt Weaver, friends and colleagues at Washington & Jefferson College. I am particularly indebted to Professor Weaver for his careful reading of the manuscript and subsequent advice, and also to Jeffrey Brunner of the U. Grant Memorial Library at Washington & Jefferson College, who created the images that appear in the text. My wife Susan is my model for gracious

---

1. A partial list of their works appears in the bibliography.

Acknowledgments

living and I thank her for her ongoing support. I dedicate this book to Ryan Charles, newly born yet filled with promise and grace.

Introduction

Central Idea: The purpose of life is happiness conducive to the equitable flourishing of all living beings on planet earth.

Key Biblical Passages: Genesis 1:1; Matthew 10:16; Luke 6:32–36; 10:29–37; Romans 12:4–8; 1 Corinthians 12:7; 13:13[1]

IN THE BEGINNING . . . GOD! THAT'S a religious statement. In the beginning . . . energy! That's a scientific statement.

Are the concepts "God" and "energy" compatible, contradictory, or simply unrelated? The answer, it seems, depends upon one's conception of God and one's view of the relationship between religion and science. If God is viewed as rational being and therefore as personal, like humans are personal, and energy is viewed as non-rational and therefore as impersonal, then the gap between theological and scientific ontology appears to be great. But if God is viewed as Spirit or as life force, the gap diminishes, though not entirely, for the religious worship of God, however conceptualized, loses appeal if the object of that worship, however anthropomorphized, is by nature impersonal and random, lacking in purpose and intentionality.

When one approaches the issues of cosmic origins and cosmic essence, it is important to clarify that the biblical starting point found in Genesis 1:1 is not "In the beginning God" but "In the beginning God created." While this "event," whether called "the creation" or the "Big Bang," may be considered the primal "singularity," in the sense of the emergence of the

---

1. The verses listed here and at the start of every chapter are provided as a summary of biblical texts referenced or cited in that particular chapter. They are not intended to be studied separately or out of context.

space-time continuum, it is not a reference to an absolute starting point to reality, but rather to the primordial creative spark.

Neither science nor religion considers this "event" to be the absolute starting point to reality, for both viewpoints posit that something cannot come from nothing. The Bible assumes the preexistence of God, and science points to the First Law of Thermodynamics, which declares that energy cannot come from nothing. In either case, God/energy is either eternal in nature or must come from a preceding cause or Prime Mover, which monotheists call "God." Setting semantics aside, we have arrived at a starting point held in common by scientists and religionists alike: the primal essence of the universe, however conceived, whether personal or impersonal, whether life force or energy force, should be understood as being eternal, meaning it has no beginning and probably no end.

The Goodness of Life

This world teams with life, thanks to nature and its abundance. The rain falls on every creature, and the sun warms us all. There is a pattern and order to nature that when acknowledged proves to be both generous and hopeful. Humans, following nature, have adopted patterns and rituals that create boundaries and therefore order and meaning to their lives, expressed in families and neighborhoods, societies and nations, and in global citizenship. We have settled into jobs and careers and have devised disciplines, ideologies, religions, arts, technologies, and recreational activities to express our hopes and creative imagination as well as to meet our social, physical, and emotional needs. Life is so good, in fact, that humans have devised ways to enhance and prolong it.

Despite great abundance, nature's goodness seems threatened these days by human waste, negligence, and consumption. If we continue to live arrogantly, selfishly, wastefully, and suspiciously, addicted to violence, chemicals, and hedonistic pursuits, and if we continue to view others as enemies or as inferiors, then the future of humanity and of this planet is bleak. It is not yet too late to change, but if we don't change our attitudes and lifestyles, and do not do so soon, we may reach a hopeless point of no return.

Introduction

The Good Life

Since the beginning of time, every generation has questioned whether there is a purpose to life, a point to it all. While many people today are skeptical, feeling that life is futile or meaningless, the purpose of religion and philosophy is to posit answers to life's big questions. In a previous book, I pondered this issue and concluded that *the purpose of life is to experience Life, for those who experience life fully experience God, who is Life.*[2] I now wish to modify that statement, adding moral categories to my definition: *The purpose of life is happiness conducive to the equitable flourishing of all, for God is in all.*[3] In what follows I will support the claim that we live in a moral universe and that happiness can be achieved by following specific ethical principles.

Most human beings desire a good life. Thinking about a good life, how to achieve, maintain, and enhance it, occupies a great deal of our time and attention: we build comfortable homes and secure futures for ourselves; we work hard to advance in our careers; we seek to improve our health and expand our minds; we seek satisfying and enduring relationships with people who value similar goals and activities we enjoy. And because we live in community with others, we think about people whose lives have been shaken by war or violence or natural disasters, and we wonder how their needs relate to our lives.

Although Western ethical concerns have traditionally been voiced in Christian language, we know that this search for inner peace, integrity in relationships, and genuine care for other people is widely shared by our neighbors, whether or not they are Christian. While many people today, religious or secular, think of "the good life" in terms espoused by popular culture, namely as a life built around pleasant and interesting experiences,

2. Vande Kappelle, *Beyond Belief*, xviii.

3. Though I do not believe in a "personal" God, that is, in a God understandable to human beings and essentially viewed as an "overbig" person, I am not averse to using the term "God." The Bible, both in the Jewish and Christian testaments, declare that "God is Spirit," not person. It was with a metaphysical tradition of personhood in fourth-century Greek theology that calling God "person" took on some meaning. Today, because few of us are metaphysicians of that tradition, we would be better off dropping the notion of the personhood of God and finding a deeper understanding. When we cling to the concept of God as "person," we diminish God's transcendence. Monotheism is to God what a trunk is to a tree. We deceive ourselves if we imagine that the tree is the trunk or that the trunk, being the most visible element of the tree, is therefore the most vital. The tree would be nothing without its roots, which are diverse and rarely visible. In thinking of God, I suggest two metaphors: God is both everywhere to us, like water to fish, but also God is nowhere, like "the void" and "the silence."

with enough money and leisure to meet personal desires and familial needs, few thoughtful people try to live a good life on entirely selfish terms. In fact, most of our neighbors of other faiths or of no faith would agree that the good life must include a concern for the wellbeing of others, peace between nations, and the health of our planet.

For Christians, this general understanding is sharpened by the teachings and example of Jesus, who often took generally accepted obligations and pushed them a step further, beyond what we originally thought. If the teachings of Jesus tell us about what makes a life good, they indicate that it sometimes involves putting the good of others ahead of our own:

> If you love those who love you, what credit is that to you? For even sinners love those who love them. If you do good to those who do good to you, what credit is that to you? For even sinners do the same. If you lend to those from whom you hope to receive, what credit is that to you? Even sinners lend to sinners, to receive as much again. But love your enemies, do good, and lend, expecting nothing in return. Your reward will be great, and you will be children of the Most High; for he is kind to the ungrateful and the wicked. Be merciful, just as your Father is merciful. (Luke 6:32–36)

Augustine, in his classic work *The City of God*, imagined humanity divided between two allegiances, one to an earthly or human city and the other to the City of God. The choice between them is absolute, and there can be no middle ground. The two cities are created by two kinds of love: the earthly city, created by self-love, and the City of God, created by the love of God and hence by love for "the Other" (whether conceived as "God," nature, or the stranger in need). In the Bible, the ideal of compassion for the person in need is powerfully illustrated in the parable of the Good Samaritan, found in Luke 10:29–37. Clearly, this business of living a good life is not easy. It cannot be done simply by seeking what is obviously good for oneself. But caring about the good of other people is not simply a matter of helping them get what they say they want. It may involve standing for values that will arouse their misunderstanding and disturb their peace.

Alongside the Christian's love for God, there is the biblical witness that God loves us. The Bible as a whole bears witness to the goodness of creation and its fitness for human habitation. If this is a world created as a place for human life, then our search for a good life has to be shaped in the context of a world that is shaped by love. As Robin Lovin indicates in his primer on Christian ethics, "Belief in God as the creator of a good world is less a narrative of how the world came into being than it is a fundamental confidence that we can live our lives in harmony with the natural world around us. . . . The search for a good life is not a struggle to wrest peace and happiness from a hostile or indifferent universe. Belief that God has created us for life in this world suggests also that human good is achieved by . . . a common life in which we may achieve a greater good together than any of us controls alone."[4]

Setting Goals: Shaping Our Choices and Actions

While we spend much of our time seeking a good life, we do not often think about the good life in general, or about where we want our choices to take us. Goal-setting is essential to the good life. However, in setting goals, we need to avoid being so distracted by the multitude of decisions to make that our attention is confined to specific goals.

The importance of setting goals is most apparent in our places of work. Businesses develop strategic plans for their operations, and managers determine goals that are measurable and achievable. They then communicate these goals to every part of the business, so that the goals become part of everyone's work. This goal setting has also become an expectation in nonprofit organizations, which often formulate mission statements for volunteers and employees and for a wider community of supporters. The point of a mission statement is to formulate the ways that will allow an organization to be specific and selective about its goals. In this manner every group to which we belong, from the places where we work to the places where we worship, urge us to keep our goals before us, to shape our choices and actions in the present around where we want or think we can be in the future.

This book and its subject matter functions as a mission statement for human life in the twenty-first century, for it addresses the choices we make as humans and the goals we set to safeguard not only the survival of the human race but also the health of our planet and the wellbeing of all creatures, ensuring that our best days lie ahead. The options before us are many, and the choices sometimes deeply troubling to conscientious individuals. Christian ethics says that it makes a difference what we do with the powers and opportunities at our disposal. Can we act responsibly in choosing which commitments to make?

---

4. Lovin, *Christian Ethics*, 13.

The appropriate way to regard one's abilities and opportunities, as Paul argues in Romans, is to see them as gifts: "We have gifts that differ according to the grace given to us: prophecy, in proportion to faith; ministry, in ministering; the teacher, in teaching; the exhorter, in exhortation; the giver, in generosity; the leader, in diligence; the compassionate, in cheerfulness (Rom. 12:4–8). This diversity of gifts is for the common good; they are to be used and shared (1 Cor. 12:7).

We make choices about how we use our gifts, but those choices are subject to a wider judgment. In the Bible two principles seem to govern that judgment:

- the principle of stewardship
- the principle of community

The principle of stewardship indicates that what we have in the way of opportunities, abilities, and resources are not simply ours to use and discard. Rather we are to care for these gifts and try to increase them. This has obvious implications for the way we use material goods and for how we treat the environment. In choosing our goals, we should consider "not simply the easiest and most immediate results, but those achievements that will make a larger and more lasting difference in our lives and in the lives of those around us."[5]

The principle of community enjoins us "to think about how our gifts can be used for the benefit of others. The aim is not simply peaks of individual achievement but a community in which the pursuit of our individual goals also enables others to live a good life."[6] In a moral life guided by the principles of stewardship and community, choices represent commitment to others, our goals connecting to theirs. Christian faith binds us to others and commits us to projects larger than our own.

People of faith are aware that God may interrupt their plans and send them in a new direction, but we cannot change direction unless we are already going somewhere. And unless our goals and what we perceive to be God's goals are not connected *in action*, those goals cannot be considered "moral," no matter how large they may be in our thinking and dreaming.

---

5. Ibid., 30.
6. Ibid., 31.

Introduction

Adopting a Mission Statement

As we examine Christian ethics, whether individually or in study groups, I encourage you to adopt a motto or mission statement about how you will become an agent of hope and reconciliation in your daily routine, enacting attitudes and making changes that will have positive effects on our society and be beneficial for the planet and the rest of humanity.

With that intent in mind, I present my personal mission statement:

> I endeavor to live joyously, gratefully, and graciously on this earth, valuing every opportunity at hand and every encounter with others as a gift from God and as a means of loving God. Inspired by a vision of global wellbeing, embodied in creation spirituality[7] and empowered by the principles of faith, hope, and love, I devote myself to that vision, imparting its elements and implementing its benefits.

While writing a mission statement is a valuable exercise, if the concepts are theoretical or overly grandiose, they may be impractical or unattainable. Like so many New Year's resolutions, such statements of purpose are soon forgotten, the seed falling on rocky soil or failing to grow due to neglect. To achieve their goals, missional people often align with missional organizations, joining churches or para-church groups that seek to practice their faith in the world. The results are beneficial for recipients but also transformative for participants. People who join missional organizations find their vision enlarged, their faith reinforced, and their commitment to others strengthened.

Living Virtuously

Humans are happiest when they live virtuously. This is the premise of all of the world's living religions, as well as a core principle in organizations such as the Girl and Boy Scouts of America, among the nation's oldest and most influential youth organizations. Regrettably, this movement is in decline today. However, its principles, as proclaimed in the Scout Oath and in the

---

7. Creation spirituality, a theological paradigm developed by Matthew Fox, emphasizes the original goodness of creation and the role of blessing in nature rather than the fall/redemption paradigm, which emphasizes the role of sin and evil in nature. Creation spirituality is discussed in chapter 3.

Boy and Girl Scout Laws, remain untarnished, and if practiced, would impact society profoundly.

Scout Oath: On my honor, I will do my best to do my duty to God and my country, and to obey the Scout Law; to help other people at all times; to keep myself physically strong, mentally awake, and morally straight.

Girl Scout Law: I will do my best to be honest and fair, friendly and helpful, considerate and caring, courageous and strong, and responsible for what I say and do, and to respect myself and others, respect authority, use resources wisely, make the world a better place, and be a sister to every Girl Scout.

Boy Scout Law: A Scout is trustworthy, loyal, helpful, friendly, courteous, kind, obedient, cheerful, thrifty, brave, clean, and reverent.

Many fraternal organizations exist in our world, promoting virtuous behavior. While many members join because they wish to live by high principles and ideals, others join for companionship or to promote agendas for personal success. While it is not always possible to live consistently, in the Bible we find a principle that commends balanced thinking and living. In Matthew 10:16, Jesus exhorts his disciples to "be wise as serpents and innocent as doves." What Jesus meant when he told his followers to live and witness in this manner is the subject of our study.

According to a long-standing tradition in Christianity, there are seven virtues. Four are called "natural" or "cardinal" (the word "cardinal" comes from a Latin word meaning "the hinge on the door"), signifying that they go back to the origins of human civilization and as such are recognized by all cultures as "pivotal" to moral behavior. These four—prudence, temperance, justice, and fortitude—represent how human beings can and should behave toward themselves and others. According to Thomas Aquinas, the great medieval theologian, these four virtues God expects us to attain, out of our own human resources. In that respect they represent "natural" human ability at its best.

In 1 Corinthians 13:13, the apostle Paul presents three additional qualities, so eternal and enduring that theologians have grouped them under the category of "theological" virtues: faith, hope, and love. These virtues, transcending ordinary human activity such as devotion, optimism, and kindness, are considered divine gifts for they are viewed as originating with God and as attainable only with divine assistance.[8] Because they are said to come from God, and to distinguish them from natural virtues, we will regularly refer to them as supernatural gifts. Christian authorities

---

8. For the author's sermon on 1 Corinthians 13, see appendix C.

INTRODUCTION

believed these virtues were not natural to human beings in their fallen state, but were conferred at baptism.

Chapters 5–9 examine these seven virtues individually and by category, viewing their promissory role as social, moral, and spiritual building blocks, and the theological (supernatural) virtues in particular as symbolic of a deeper metaphysical ontology.[9]

Summary

The starting point for our study is the premise that we live in a sacred universe. This perspective challenges us to think about the purpose of life, which, the author suggests, is to find happiness for ourselves and to promote the happiness of all living beings. To accomplish this goal, it is helpful for individuals to formulate personal mission statements, governed by the principles of stewardship and community. Humans are happiest when they live virtuously, guided by seven foundational virtues.

For Discussion and Reflection

1. Do you agree with the premise that life is good? Why or why not?
2. What is your understanding of God? Do you view God as personal, impersonal, or as both? Support your answer.

---

9. When we think metaphysically, most of us think dualistically, using paired opposites such as good and evil, light and darkness, male and female, and yin and yang to depict reality, but this way of seeing places limits on our understanding. To expand our horizons, Christian scholar Cynthia Bourgeault suggests that we replace binary systems with ternary perspectives, adding a third "mediating" or "reconciling" principle to the mix. For instance, instead of focusing on man and woman, emphasizing man, woman, and child, and instead of envisioning black or white, seeing black, white, and gray. This principle is evident in the Christian Trinity, with the incarnated Christ as its culminating expression. According to this perspective, the third force is not a product of the first two, as in the classic Hegelian synthesis, but is independent and coequal with the others. The interweaving of the three produces a fourth force or realm of possibility. In contrast to binary systems, which seek completion in stability, through the balance of opposites, ternary perspectives create a synthesis at a whole new level, seeking completion in newness. In *The Holy Trinity and the Law of Three*, Bourgeault advises that we not limit this metaphysical principle to one triad (Father, Son, and Holy Spirit), but rather that we envision the Holy Trinity as one of many triads, each revealing different facets of the divine wholeness.

3. If God can be said to be the ultimate source of goodness, how can this be substantiated?

4. Do you agree that the purpose of life is to find and maximize happiness on planet earth? Support your answer.

5. Do you believe that life has a purpose? If so, write a statement that best summarizes your view or understanding of life's purpose.

6. Identify a passage from the Bible that best sums up the purpose of life.

7. In your own words, summarize your understanding of the principles of stewardship and community. Identify specific ways by which you can implement them in your life.

8. Construct a motto or mission statement about how you can become an agent of hope and reconciliation in your daily life.

Chapter 1

Cosmology, Anthropology, and Morality

Central Idea: To give meaning to existence and to promote socio-environmental wellbeing, human beings construct cosmologies.

Key Biblical Passage: John 3:16–17

ALBERT EINSTEIN WAS ONCE asked, "What is the most important question you can ask in life?" He answered, "Is the universe a friendly place or not?" In the first century AD, when Jesus lived and when the New Testament was being recorded, the most important question in the Mediterranean world was, "Are the angels friend or foe?" Since angels were understood to be the driving force behind the elements of the universe, it is clear that the people of that era wanted to know if the universe was a friendly place or not.

The early Christians had a definite response to Einstein's pressing question: The universe is a beneficent place, for it is created by a loving God, maintained by the Son, and renewed by the Spirit. This affirmation is clearly stated in John 3:16–17, a biblical passage beloved by Christians and non-Christians alike: "For God so loved the world that he gave his only Son, so that everyone who believes in him may not perish but may have eternal life. Indeed, God did not send the Son into the world to condemn the world, but in order that the world might be saved through him." The First Christians came to this conviction about the nature of reality through their experience with the incarnated Christ, who for them represented the love of God, the goodness of the universe, and sovereignty over all its powers, including the invisible angels. The Gospels and the early Christological hymns composed by first-century Christians celebrate the power of Jesus Christ over all dominions, visible and invisible.

Human beings have always been fascinated with the universe, including their place in the order of things. Over time, they devised models of reality to help explain their experience and to guide their conduct. The ancient Greek philosophers were deeply interested in this endeavor, developing cosmological models to explain their understanding of reality. In the fifth century BC, two pre-Socratics, Parmenides and Heraclitus, set the stage for later thinkers, arriving at diametrical conclusions about the universe. Parmenides, a monist, argued for the unity, permanence, and eternity of reality, declaring that all things in the universe are made of one thing, which he called Being. A rationalist, he arrived at his model of the universe through reason, rather than through the senses, which he distrusted. Heraclitus, an empiricist, focused on change and diversity in the universe. His observations led him to conclude that there is no permanence, for everything changes. As he put it, "no one steps into the same river twice." Unlike Parmenides, whose focus was on Being, Heraclitus was concerned with Becoming.

Two successors, Plato and Aristotle, championed their concerns, developing comprehensive views of reality. Plato's model, the first grand synthesis, explained permanence and change dualistically. Plato posited two realms to reality, the Physical World, consisting of "particulars" (temporary things such as trees, horses, chairs, and triangles), which are always in flux, and the Ideal World, consisting of "universals" (ideals, essences, or "forms" such as treeness, horseness, chairness, and triangularity), which are eternal and unchanging. Concerned with permanence (Being), Plato viewed objects in the Physical World as copies of forms in the ideal world.

In Plato's Ideal World, forms were related hierarchically, meaning there were lesser forms (such as treeness and triangularity), intermediate forms (such as beauty and justice), and a supreme form or highest ideal, which Plato called The Good. Using a mathematical model for reality, Plato ingeniously combined the views of Parmenides (Being) and Heraclitus (Becoming), creating a model that demonstrated the superiority of permanence over change.

Aristotle, Plato's pupil, seeking unity *in* the universe, disagreed with Plato's dualistic approach, using a biological model to explain how things can change, yet remain the same. Aristotle claimed there was only one reality—the physical—arguing that the form (essence) of a particular thing is within the object. Using analogies from nature such as how acorns become oak trees, he explained that what changes is the matter, but not the form of an object. Building on the principle of Becoming, Aristotle postulated that all things change, going from potentiality to actuality, and that all motion or change originates with a Prime Mover or a First Cause, which he called the Unmoved Mover. For Aristotle, this first cause of motion was itself unmoved, unchanged, and unalterable.

Later scientists—Ptolemy, Copernicus, Newton, Einstein—contributed substantially to Western cosmology, thereby creating a series of shifts in worldview known successively as Ptolemaic, Copernican, Newtonian, and Einsteinium. Curiously, each view contradicted the previous understanding of the cosmos. While initially resisted as heretical, each eventually became acceptable, replacing the previous mindset. Like the narrative of the history of life on earth, the story of the cosmic universe continues to be revised, its portrait redrawn.

The current age is fraught with uncertainty; even experts disagree on the nature of reality. Since the birth of modern science in the seventeenth century, essential hypotheses concerning the cosmic universe and the history of life on earth have been abandoned, and our understanding of reality continues to be revised. Affirming that scientists cannot explain how nature behaves the way it does, postmodern science presents not another model of the universe, but no model at all.

Despite the contributions and improvements of modern science, its ability to provide us with a worldview is limited, for we now know that science is limited to that part of the world that is physical, calculable, and testable. We cannot look to science to tell us about realities such as God, soul, and the like, for science now declares itself limited with respect to the invisible. Large parts of the universe (some say 90 percent of the scientist's universe; others posit as high as 99 percent) are at present invisible. Protons, for example, derive from photons, and photons are only "virtually" real; they have no rest mass, lose no energy to the mediums they traverse, and are not objectively detectable because they are annihilated upon being perceived. Using instruments such as atomic particle colliders, scientists are conceding that invisibles exist and also that these invisibles precede the visible and in some way give rise to it.

Physicists at the Large Hadron Collider, located beneath the France-Switzerland border, are now embarking on the quest to probe some of the biggest puzzles about the universe, such as dark matter and the possible presence of other dimensions or universes, as postulated by "string theory." These scientists have greatly increased knowledge of the Higgs boson, the invisible particle responsible for giving other elementary particles mass. Without this particle, known as the "God particle," the universe would be cold, dark, and lifeless. Data from this collider have also confirmed the existence of quarks, tiny ingredients that make up subatomic particles such as proton and neutrons, and proved the existence of mesons, unstable particles found in cosmic rays (consisting of one quark and one antiquark).

According to Paul Dirac, the father of antimatter, "All matter is created out of some imperceptible substratum. This substratum is not accurately described as material, since it uniformly fills all space and is undetectable by any observation. In a sense it appears as nothingness—immaterial, undetectable, and omnipresent. But it is a peculiar form of nothingness, out of which all matter is created."[1]

In his 1976 book, *Forgotten Truth*, the renowned scholar of comparative religions, Huston Smith, delves into the "primordial tradition," the common, fundamental experience of humankind, as found in the core teachings of the world's religions, identifying therein a cosmology based on the idea of an ontological gradation of reality.

According to Smith, the "primordial tradition" is perhaps best distinguished by its recognition of the many-layered nature of both reality and the self. Smith narrows these layers to four: reality is composed of the terrestrial, intermediate, celestial, and infinite levels, while the self is composed of the body, mind, soul, and spirit, as depicted in the following diagram:[2]

---

1. This summary of Dirac's position is cited in Smith, *Forgotten Truth*, 115–16.
2. Smith's diagram appears on page 62 of *Forgotten Truth*.

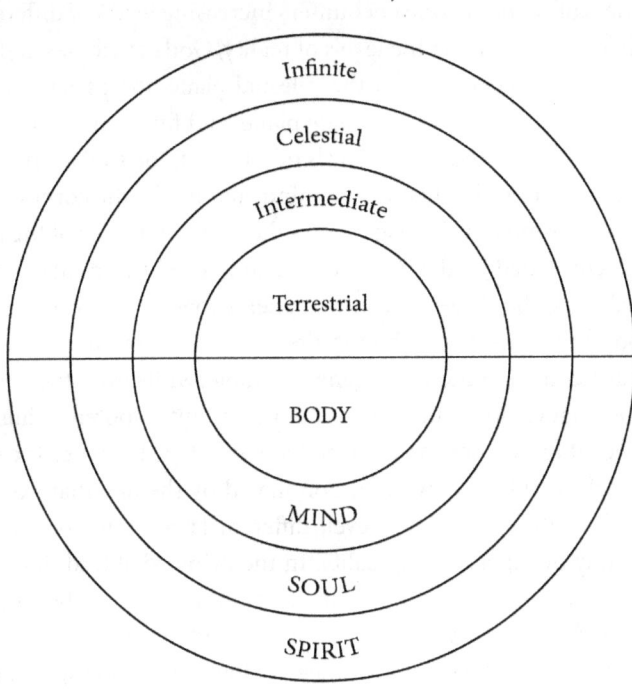

Levels of Reality / Levels of Selfhood

These tiers correlate in such a way that higher levels of reality correspond to deeper levels of the self:

- the terrestrial tier (also called the material, physical, sensible, corporeal, and phenomenal) corresponds to the body;
- the intermediate tier (also called the subtle, psychic, or astral) corresponds to the mind;
- the celestial tier (this realm views God as personal; here one speaks of God's attributes and personality) corresponds to the soul;
- the Infinite tier (this realm views God as transpersonal; this level is best spoken of through analogy, in negative terms, or through paradox) corresponds to the Spirit.

The highest and deepest tiers, Infinite and Spirit, are, according to Smith, without limitation; while the Infinite is unbounded externally, the human Spirit is unbounded internally. These two (undifferentiated) levels, therefore, are in fact the same. As one moves down the tiers of reality and out the tiers of selfhood, one encounters increasing levels of differentiation and/or materialization: on the levels of reality, God's attributes and personality as well as "archetypes" on the celestial plane, the psychic reflections of the archetypes on the intermediate plane, and finally material reality on the terrestrial plane; and on the levels of selfhood, the soul as the source of mind and locus of individuality, the mind, and finally the corporeal body.

Smith's cosmological image shows the earth, symbolic of the terrestrial sphere, enveloped by the intermediate sphere, which in turn is enclosed by the celestial, the three concentric spheres together superimposed on a background that represents the Infinite. "Considered in itself, each sphere appears as a complete and homogeneous whole, while from the perspective of the area that encloses and permeates it, it is but a content. Thus the terrestrial world knows not the intermediate world, or the latter the celestial, though each world is known and dominated by the one that exceeds and enfolds it."[3] With each higher level, different laws apply, together with a different way of experiencing reality. In the primordial tradition, the possibility exists that one of the higher metaphysical levels can "break through" into one of the lower levels, in so doing overriding the laws of that lower level. By definition, the laws of science are limited in their application primarily to the physical (terrestrial) level.

Whereas Smith places the body in the innermost circle, as the most accessible aspect, with the other levels expanding concentrically outward to the spirit, humanity's most expansive element, I think of the body as the outermost level, the container for the inner levels of selfhood. I begin with the body and emphasize its role for two reasons: (a) to counter longstanding religious misrepresentations of the body as the place and cause of sin, and (b) to highlight the body's vital role in spiritual health. One of the great tragedies of religious history occurred when the physical body was falsely accused for the sins of humanity. The idea that our most basic bodily functions, including our sensual pleasure and sexual passion, are unclean and unholy is not only a regrettable belief system, it is also profoundly ignorant. In her book *The Seeker's Guide*, Elizabeth Lesser affirms that "[d]eep spirituality is not an out-of-body experience; it's an in-body experience."[4]

Body and mind are not separate; neither are body and emotions or body and soul. Humans are not spiritual beings trapped in a carnal

---

3. Ibid., 61.
4. Lesser, *Seeker's Guide*, 242.

existence. The self is like a diamond, each part a facet of the same essence. When we view our bodies as base and vulgar and our souls and spirits as pure and distinct, we affirm dualism, the bane of spirituality. If we recognize our bodies to be "materialized spirit," and therefore spiritually based, we are on our way to wholeness and truth. Care of the body, therefore, is the first and most important principle of religion. If we are to make spiritual progress, we must learn to love and care for our bodies. This is the starting premise of all healthy spirituality.

Moving inward from body we come to mind, the seat of consciousness, conceived as distinct from the brain, which is part of the body. The mind is not our thoughts, but rather a container for life's continual creative impulses. According to Smith, there is no convincing materialistic explanation of mind, for mind cannot be measured quantitatively. Furthermore, mind conforms to laws that differ in kind from those that matter exemplifies.

The third level of selfhood is the soul (called by ancients *psyche*, *anima*, *atman*, *nephesh*, or *nafs*), the final locus of our individuality, its source and yet superior. The soul is closer to our essence than is the mind, with which we usually identify. While the soul is finite, it is the only possible bridge to Spirit, the fourth level of selfhood. If soul is the element in humans that relates to God, Spirit is the element that is identical with God, not with God's personal mode but with God's mode that is infinite. Mystics and theologians speak of identity at this level because here the subject-object dichotomy is transcended." While Spirit is infinite, humans remain finite because they are not Spirit only. Our specifically human overlay—body, mind, and soul—is said to veil the Spirit within us.

The key point in Smith's model is the realization that as far as selfhood is concerned, one cannot maintain harmony, equilibrium, and flow by jumping across levels. Each level builds consecutively and concentrically on the preceding. In other words, the bridge to consciousness is the body. To understand the mind, one must be fully grounded in one's physicality. The link to soul is mind, and the link to Spirit is soul. Each level must be explored deeply and authentically before it can serve as conduit to the next. To acquire meaning and understanding, one cannot jump from body to soul or from mind to Spirit. For Smith, the final link, the door that leads from soul to spirit, is love: "For Spirit to permeate the self's entirety, the components of the self must be aligned: body in temperance, mind in understanding, and soul in love."[5]

5. Ibid., 92.

In his book *Why Religion Matters*, Huston Smith touches on his theory of spiritual personality types. These types have little to do with an individual's actual beliefs, but rather focus on how individuals approach those beliefs. There are four types: the Atheist, the Polytheist, the Monotheist, and the Mystic.

The Atheist lacks any one center of value and power of sufficient transcendence to focus and order life, and hence is unconcerned with God. If the Atheist goes to church, it is primarily a social exercise or an aesthetic appreciation of the rituals themselves. Atheists may or may not follow the moral and social dictates of an ecclesiastical tradition, but if they do, it is only because they agree with their own conclusions.

The Polytheist, like the atheist, also lacks a center of value and power sufficient to focus and order life. Having "interests" in many minor centers of value and power, his or her commitments tend to be transient and shifting. The Polytheist is primarily concerned with lesser spiritual being in the world (angels, saints, demons). In the case of some Christians, while they acknowledge the supremacy of God, the focus of spiritual practice is not God but the saints, angels, or demons. Polytheists see the influence of these beings everywhere. They believe that demons tempt us and angels protect us, and they are much more likely to pray to saints than to God. Such people tend to be laid back in terms of commitment or trust.[6]

Unlike the Atheist or the Polytheist, *the Monotheist* focuses trust and loyalty in a transcendent center of value and power. While acknowledging the spirits that define the Polytheist's worldview, the Monotheist focuses on God, praying to God, not the saints. Monotheists may believe in Satan and in demonic influence, but they are untroubled by this. Radical monotheistic faith rarely finds long-lasting actualization in limited, parochial communities, for people who do so tend to lapse into confusing temporal representations of transcendence with that reality itself.

The Mystic finds God in everything; even Satan is viewed ultimately as God's creature. The mystic is likely to have a well-developed theodicy, and does not pray so much as seek communion with God. Mystics may be extremely observant, practicing the rituals and adhering to the beliefs of the Church, or they may forge their own path in moral and doctrinal matters.

---

6. Most of us are more polytheistic that we might like to think. The practical impact of our consumer society's dominant myth—that you should experience and own everything you desire—makes the polytheist pattern seem normative.

For Smith, people differ in metaphysical capacity not because they are superior or morally better than those of another type but simply due to differences in ability, akin to someone having mathematical or musical aptitude. Everything the materialist sees, the polytheist sees, with other things added. On the third level, the vision of polytheism coalesces in or under the God of monotheism—the Great Spirit. Finally, the monotheistic God gives way to the unfathomable, indescribable mystery of the mystic—the Godhead or the ineffable Infinite.

The Starting Point for Understanding Reality

Cosmology, defined as the study of the nature of the cosmos, including its origin and essence, underlies all that is of consequence in society, including economics, politics, morality, spirituality, and theology. As an academic discipline, cosmology can be apprehended either scientifically—as a field of study related to explanations of the origins and evolution of the universe—or anthropologically—as an interpretive framework concerned with the role and meaning of human life and the world.

Thus, when physicists and astronomers study cosmology, they refer to a field of science or to a scientific process, whereas when anthropologists explore cosmology, they contemplate how society contemplates its relation to humanity, life, the earth, and the cosmos. In anthropology, a cosmology involves explanations about the past, present, and future and deals with origins as well as the destiny of a society and of humanity within the broader whole. It is an anthropological approach that we take here, particularly its relation to a religious and ethical interpretive framework.

All cultures have cosmologies, either religious or non-religious in nature, as means to interpret a society's role in the universe, earth, biosphere, and within humanity. While individuals and groups use their cosmologies to define the meaning of human existence within humanity and also within the greater universe, the response differs if there is a religion or spiritual approximation to supply the questions and answers to these matters. While cosmologies can remain static, particularly in traditional societies, they can also change along an individual's life cycle and according to one's expertise, gender, and status.

Anthropologists agree that there are overarching systems that provide meaning to human existence within the grander world and universe. Whereas secular anthropologists speak of cognitive and behavioral universals which humans may use to manufacture cosmologies, religious anthropologists point to spiritual parameters, holding supernatural factors to be key parts of existence. For theistic anthropologists, the agency of God runs the universe, the world, and also human destiny.

Rapid change and modernity are engulfing most societies nowadays, threatening treasured values, worldviews, and perspectives, and modern societies are caught in a struggle to maintain their cosmologies while respecting or marginalizing those of others. Progressive factions within those societies increasingly favor novelty and diversity, transposing existing cosmologies or fabricating new ones.

Due to the advances of science, which affect us all, there is a significant amount of knowledge about the origins and evolution of the universe, and of its laws, forces, and structure and composition. However, the vast majority of people, even in the Western world, do not apply this modern scientific cosmology into their personal cosmology.

Recently, among concerned scientists, ecologically minded philosophers, ethicists, theologians, and religious practitioners, a significant process is occurring, where there appears to be an upgrading of cosmological referents to engage in socio-environmental ethics and also in quests to achieve human wellbeing, justice, and equity, whether in non-religious or in spiritual approximation, including a sense of responsibility toward nature. There is also a concern to adopt a new paradigm for sustainability, one which considers people as part of nature rather than as opposed to it. In such cosmologies, knowing more about the universe, nature, earth, humanity, and the question of purpose and meaning is vital.

This knowledge and understanding can enhance a consciousness of the interdependencies between humanity, ecosystems, and the climate, and can help to correct the short-sighted, risk-prone human activities that are degrading ecosystems, exterminating biodiversity, augmenting consumerism, increasing human population and social inequity, intensifying the use of fossil fuels, and accelerating climate change, together with other human actions that in a historically unprecedented manner are endangering human survival itself.

As globalization is accompanied by wars (including wars of cosmologies) and by rising financial and economic crises (including soaring food prices and the impacts of climate change), the dynamics relating cosmologies to cultures will increasingly become pivotal not only in the configuration of humankind's profile, but of its own existence and that of a large part of life.

Cosmology and Morality

When we think of morality, we think of behaving fairly and harmoniously with those around us, often by following values or standards provided by family members, teachers, religious figures, and the media, or acquired through trial and error or from peers.

Ultimately, however, we arrive at the question of the general purpose of human life, and to the beliefs we hold about the universe, God, human origins, and the afterlife. Such views have a philosophical and theological nature and often are the byproducts of religious education and upbringing. For Christians, morality is often based on scriptural teachings such as the Ten Commandments and the Golden Rule.

For the remainder of this book I assume Christian perspectives on morality, theology, and cosmology, interpreting them in ways that are compatible with the discoveries of science and the teachings of the world's major religions.

Summary

To discover purpose and meaning in life, human beings must discern whether they live in a beneficent universe. This raises cosmological and anthropological questions regarding the nature of the universe and the place of humans in the order of things. Philosophical and scientific cosmological models, such as Huston Smith's intriguing model, correlate the multi-layered nature of reality and the self. People differ in metaphysical outlook, as shown by Smith's theory of spiritual personality types, their views on reality profoundly influencing their ecclesiastical rituals and practices.

For Discussion and Reflection

1. What is your answer to Einstein's question? Is the universe a friendly place or not?

2. Do you agree with the Christian response to Einstein's question? Why or why not?

3. In your own words, state your understanding of Plato's and Aristotle's cosmological perspectives. Which do you find more compelling? Why?

4. In your estimation, why do human construct cosmologies? Do you agree with the negative postmodern assessment concerning models of the universe?

5. Do you find Huston Smith's diagram useful? Why or why not?

6. What merits and shortcomings do you find in his theory of spiritual personality types?

7. In your own words, discuss the differences between scientific and anthropological cosmological approaches in terms of scope and methodology.

8. What advantages and disadvantages do you find in scientific cosmologies? In anthropological models?

Chapter 2

The Role of Religion

Central Idea: The role of religion is to unify people, not to divide them.

Key Biblical Passages: Genesis 12:3; Exodus 15:2; Leviticus 19:18; Deuteronomy 6:4; Mark 12:30–31

THE ROLE OF RELIGION, whether in formulating a worldview or in shaping a lifestyle, has until recently been considered indispensable. Religion is one of several systems devised by humans to provide guidance and meaning to the whole order of existence. The phenomenon of religion has been pervasive throughout the history of humanity and continues to be central to most cultures of the world. The role of religion in the current clash between cultures, whether viewed through a secular, traditional, or fundamentalist lens, is enormous, and any headway we are able to make in the future in terms of peace and international cooperation will involve moral principles that value and encourage ecumenical understanding and inter-religious dialogue.

Avoiding Dualistic Frameworks

If religion is central to culture, there should be agreement among scholars on a definition of religion, but no consensus exists. In order to provide distinction between religion and non-religion, some scholars appeal to a distinction between two realms of reality, the sacred and the secular, arguing that human involvement with the sacred defines the essence of religion.

The notion that religion can be defined as human interaction with the sacred has a long legacy in the West. This view, based upon a sacred-secular dualism, divides the world into two domains, the one containing all that is sacred and the other all that is profane. This understanding of religion was advanced and popularized in the middle of the twentieth century in Mircea Eliade's classic work *The Sacred and the Profane: The Nature of Religion*.

This distinction, based on an antiquated dualistic perspective long entrenched in the Western mindset, provides insuperable problems for many modern individuals, whose experience leads them to conceptualize the sacred (and therefore the supernatural, the spiritual, the metaphysical, and the nonmaterial) as a projection and/or an extension of society, thereby collapsing the sacred into the profane (the natural, physical, and material). This approach, while appearing reductionist, need not be dismissive of the sacred as a purely human construct. The intention can be cautionary about the inherent problems with the sacred-profane dualism and instructive in noting that this dualistic worldview is not a universal idea but a particularly Western construction.

Religion as Noun or as Adjective

John Esposito, longtime professor and author of texts on world religions, highlights the difficulty of defining the term "religion" by asking his readers to engage in a thought experiment.[1] Suppose you could enter a time machine, he suggests, and be transported back to the city of Rome in the first century. He selects ancient Rome because the word "religion" has its roots in the Latin language of the Roman Empire, and also because understanding how the Romans used the word might help us define what we mean by the term religion today.

Imagine that you are walking down a street in ancient Rome, and you approach a group of people standing on a corner. You ask: "What religion are you?" but they seem puzzled by the question. They understand the individual words, but the phrasing seems awkward and they do not understand what you are asking. So you rephrase the question: "Are you religious?" This causes them to smile and reply, "Of course, isn't everyone?"

Why did they understand the second question but not the first?

According to Esposito, the first question treats the word religion as a noun describing distinct social bodies, such that each person understands

---

1. Esposito et al., *World Religions Today*, 5–7.

himself or herself as identifying with and belonging to only one of those organization; if you are a Christian, you are by definition not a Jew or a Buddhist. But this way of understanding would be foreign to a person living in antiquity, and today it is foreign to many people living in Africa and Asia. Esposito points out that in Japan even today it is possible to be Buddhist, Taoist, Confucian, and Shinto all at the same time.

Once you rephrase the question from "What religion are you?" to "Are you religious?" you shift the function of the term religion from being a noun describing a distinct social group to being an adjective describing "an attitude toward the human condition—a way of seeing, acting, and experiencing all things."[2] According to Esposito, throughout history most people did not think of religion as a noun, as a separate reality they had to choose over and against another reality.

Esposito suggests that ancient Greeks and Romans viewed religion as a way of respecting all powers, natural and supernatural, that govern one's destiny, whether they be associated with war, fertility, or other aspects of society. Of course one would want all those forces on one's side. Anything else would be disastrous. For ancient Romans, as for nearly all other people throughout history, religion was essentially about divine favor and its influence on human destiny. According to this perspective, religion is not just about "spiritual" things, or deities, or God. Rather, religious attitudes are as diverse as the forms of power that people believe govern their destiny, whether these forms of power are related to nature, wealth, political power, individual wellbeing, or the forces of history.

Esposito's emphases seem spot-on. He is certainly correct to point out that the contemporary tendency to think of religion as a noun is rather unique to the contemporary Western world and that such a view represents a departure from what has been commonly understood by most people throughout history. Also, Esposito's attempt to reframe religion as an attitude toward power, in which he includes social, political, and economic power, suggests that religion must be understood as a phenomenon pervading all of society, rather than as a distinct element existing in but separate from other elements of society.

---

2. Ibid., 6.

The Etymology of the Word "Religion"

While it is true that many societies do not draw a clear line between culture and what scholars would call "religion," this does not mean that religion doesn't exist. What it does mean is that even when we think we have a handle on what religion is, we might be off base. Perhaps the most helpful starting point in understanding religion and its role in society is to examine the etymology of the word.

The classic explanation of the word "religion," traced to the first-century BC Roman orator Cicero, derives religion from the Latin word *relegere* (*re* + *lege*), which means "to read over again," in the sense of "consider carefully." Thus *religio*, the nominative of the Latin *religionem*, came to mean such things as "respect for what is sacred, reverence for the gods, sense of right, and religious observance." Religious law maintained the proprieties of divine honors, sacrifice to the gods, and proper ritual. Incorrect ritual and improper sacrifice were *vitia* (translated as "vice" in English), and the improper use or search of divine knowledge was *superstitio*. Neglecting the *religiones* (plural of *religio*) owed to the traditional gods was considered atheism, a charge leveled by ancient Romans at Christians as well as at Jews and Epicureans. The reason was clear: any moral deviation from acceptable religious norms was not only perverse, but it could bring harm to the state.

Another possible origin of "religion" is the Latin word *religare*, which means "to tie or to bind fast." Many modern writers favor this etymology, on the assumption that it helps to explain the power inherent in religion. Modern scholar Joseph Campbell favors a derivation from *ligo* (bind, connect), probably from a prefixed *re* (again) + *ligare*, meaning "to reconnect," a correlation made prominent by Augustine, based on an interpretation by Lactantius. The question immediately arises, to what should one reconnect? The answer is not clear. To theists, *religare* means to reconnect to God and to God's will for our lives. To polytheists *religare* implies reconnecting to the higher powers around us, and to the values espoused by social and religious leaders. To nature-based cultures, *religare* means to revere nature's ways, and to find one's place in the natural order. In each case, finding harmony with that which is considered to be ultimate in power and reverence, whether natural or supernatural, and with other human beings, is essential and mandatory. For monotheists, *religare* is best expressed in the double-love command, also known as the Great Commandment: "You shall love the Lord your God with all your heart, and with all your soul, and with all your mind, and with all your strength ... and your neighbor as yourself" (Mark 12:30–31; cf. Deut. 6:4; Lev. 19:18).

A third possible origin of the term "religion" is the Latin word *religiens*, meaning "careful," in contrast to *negligens*, its opposite. In this sense, religion is a way of life lived thoughtfully and mindfully, not neglecting duties or devotion.

Because all three definitions are instructive, I recommend that you take a few moments to personalize their meaning by pondering the following questions (note that these questions also appear under question 4 at the end of this chapter):

1. What do I hold sacred in my life? How do I show respect for the sacred in my life?
2. What do I consider to be "ultimate" in the universe in terms of power and reverence? How can I find harmony with this power?
3. Am I living thoughtfully and mindfully? How do I fall short of that mark? How can I live more intentionally? Am I lacking in discipline or devotion?

A Definition of Religion

The attempt to define religion is a relatively recent phenomenon. As scholars are divided on the etymology of religion, so also they disagree on its definition. Some find the task to be impossible, arguing that attempts to define religion comprehensively inevitably fall victim to the bias of a particular religious or non-religious point of view. Others maintain that given the basic diversity among cultures and religions, no single definition encompassing all religions is possible.

Definitions of religion suffer from being either too narrow, excluding many belief systems that most agree are religious, or from being too vague and ambiguous, suggesting that practically anything qualifies as religion. A good example of a narrow definition is the common attempt to define "religion" as "belief in God," effectively excluding non-theistic views and ignoring the multiple conceptions of God held by people throughout history and even today. A good example of a vague definition is the tendency to define religion doctrinally, as a perspective or worldview. Here again it would be hard to draw a line between what qualifies as "religious" ideology or as non-religious ideology, and once again we fall into the dualistic dilemma to which we alluded earlier.

In what follows, I am not concerned with a definition that might be acceptable to everyone or applicable universally, for such a definition does not exist. Rather I employ a definition by William A. Young: "*Religion is human transformation in response to perceived ultimacy.*"[3] Notice that his definition involves two distinct phenomena: belief and behavior. Stated differently, what people believe has consequences for the way they act.

While this definition seems excessively broad, in that "ultimacy" could apply to non-religious areas of concern such as political, economic, and cultural pursuits, that is not Young's intention. His use of the concept of ultimacy carries specific meaning: "The ultimate is the center of life; it conditions and gives meaning to all of existence."[4] Other authors define religion in supportive ways. William A. Christian defines ultimate reality as something that is "more important than anything else in the universe,"[5] and Paul Tillich famously defined religion as that which is of "ultimate concern."

Young, Christian, and Tillich converge in their understanding of religion as that which leads to personal and social transformation, and that is my approach as well. The definition of religion as a "means toward ultimate transformation," initially formulated by Fred Streng in 1973, views religion as a way of life oriented to a common goal, the goal being to reach a state conceived to be the highest possible for individuals and societies.[6] "Religious" persons are said to acknowledge that life is under threat (often called sin or evil), whether by illusion, ignorance, chaos, oppression, self-destruction, or death. Whereas "religious" persons are said to acknowledge these threats because they see themselves as only potentially human, "non-religious" persons tend to think of their humanity simply as given.

In this definition, the phrase "means toward" refers to the various ways by which people seek to become changed into that highest state, individually and communally, including ethical, social, economic, mystical, and aesthetic practices and pursuits. Likewise, the phrase "ultimate transformation" implies that human life presents us with a quest or comprehensive task

---

3. Young, *World's Religion*, 3.
4. Ibid., 5.
5. Christian, *Meaning and Truth in Religion*, 60.
6. Streng et al., *Ways of Being Religious*.

(often called salvation, enlightenment, liberation or fulfillment), something non-religious persons disavow.

The Doctrine of Salvation

Many Christians have been reared with the sin and salvation paradigm, a view prominently upheld in evangelical preaching and teaching.[7] While the Christian tradition tends to present the doctrine of salvation in terms of the ultimate destiny of the individual, this is not accurate, for as the etymology of the word demonstrates, "salvation" comes from the Latin word *salutas*, meaning "security, safety, or wholeness." The majority of current Christian scholars are convinced that the modern evangelical emphasis on "being saved," which views salvation primarily as an assurance of entrance to heaven, is at best a rather recent emphasis in Christian tradition, going back no earlier than the nineteenth century. In the Bible the concept of salvation had an essentially this-worldly orientation, meaning that the concept was used to assure believers of security from physical and external threats and to guarantee their place in the coming Kingdom of God on earth. Only rarely was salvation viewed as a vehicle to transport deceased or end-time believers to a heavenly kingdom.

In the Bible, the prototypical model for salvation is the Exodus from bondage in Egypt. In the Song of Moses, a hymnic passage about the Exodus, God is proclaimed as the "salvation" of the Israelites (Exod. 15:2) because God was instrumental in their deliverance from oppression. Likewise, the story of Abraham becomes the prototypical model for the journey of faith. Scholars emphasize that the underlying significance of the patriarchal stories in Genesis is not so much the stories of the patriarchs but the story of Israel's self-understanding. At the time this material was put into writing, the main question was not, "Who are Abraham, Isaac, Jacob, and Joseph?" but "Who is Israel?" Israel was grappling with her identity, her self-understanding as a people called by God. The theological answer was found in the doctrine of election.

What does election mean? The biblical answer is given in the portrayal of Abraham, Isaac, and Jacob, patriarchs whose lives were characterized by the following traits:

---

7. This segment on sin and salvation is taken from my earlier book, *Beyond Belief*, 28–29.

a. They *lived by faith in God*. In Abraham, Israel understands something about herself, that she has been called into existence by God himself, that she has been created by God's initiative and preserved by God's grace.

b. They were *called to be a servant people*. Election does not mean that one people is chosen because they are better than others, but rather that they are called to spread God's grace. God's purpose is seen in Genesis 12:3 ("in you all the families of the earth shall be blessed"); it is a universal purpose, one that moves from particulars to universals, from individuals to communities and nations. In Abraham, God brings one person of faith into existence in order that God's blessing might be extended to all humanity. This is the Bible's stress on election, that when God calls a people, they are called to service, and the rest of the Old Testament, and then the Gospels and Epistles, show what it means to be a servant people. The Bible makes it clear that Israel's calling is part of God's healing intention (the biblical word for healing, health, wholeness, and goodness is "salvation," like the Hebrew word "Shalom"). In the Bible, the election of a people becomes the basis for good news, what the New Testament calls "gospel."

c. They were *called to a life of pilgrimage*—a life of mobility, movement, and change. Biblical faith is a calling faith, a calling to go forth, to be on the way, to be moving in God's direction, to be pioneers of faith. Abraham was told to break his ties with his land and his former security, a way of life that up to that point had been deeply rooted to the land. Like Abraham, God's people are called to a nomadic consciousness. We see that clearly in the prophetic consciousness, a stance counter-cultural in the sense that one could be both an agent of change and a critic of the established order. The prophetic message was that God was doing a new thing. As we see in Abraham, faith is not so much consent or agreement as something dynamic, manifested in movement. So Abraham is the ancestor of a pilgrim people, and his story highlights the themes of mobility and change, meaning that when faith becomes lifeless, stagnant, or frozen, whether in institutions with superiority complexes or in self-serving lifestyles, God breaks them down and forces his people into radical recommitment. The story of Abraham and the patriarchs is the story of God on the move with his people.

The doctrine of salvation is complex. During the course of church history varying aspects of the Christian understanding of sin and salvation have been emphasized by different sects and denominations as well as by theologians and teachers in specific situations. Recent studies of the biblical notion of salvation emphasize the importance of contextualization, meaning that, because the Christian gospel always addresses specific situations, the doctrine of salvation should be appropriate to those circumstances. For example, to the oppressed—whether spiritually, economically, or politically—the gospel message is that of liberation; to those burdened by personal guilt, the message is one of forgiveness; to the despondent, the message is one of hope.

Christianity holds that the created order, particularly humanity, has fallen into disorder. Things are not what they were meant to be, and something needs to be done about this. The same God who made the created order must act to reorder it, something God accomplished through the life, death, and resurrection of Jesus Christ. In his widely used text *Christian Theology*, Alistair McGrath provides answers given by Christians throughout their history to the question, "*from* what are we saved?" In each case, the doctrine of sin provides an answer. Each model, in turn, also points to the doctrine of salvation, with its hopeful answers.[8]

From what, then, are we saved? McGrath provides six answers: Christians are saved from (1) their human condition, (2) their guilt, (3) their lack of holiness, (4) their inauthentic human existence (characterized by faith in the transient material world), (5) oppression, and (6) from forces that enslave humanity—such as satanic forces, evil spirits, fear of death, or the power of sin. In summary, the Christian doctrine of salvation deals with the restoration of all things, including humanity, to its proper relationship to God.

Salvation, consequently, represents new possibilities, a new state of being. McGrath provides models of salvation that correspond to the six models of sin. Together, they answer the question, "*for* what are we saved?" Christians are saved for (1) relationship with God, (2) righteousness in the sight of God, (3) personal holiness, (4) authentic human existence, (5) social and political liberation, and (6) spiritual freedom.

The understanding of salvation presented above exhibits a radical this-worldly orientation. The reason is clear: traditional Christians followed their Jewish counterparts in placing their faith into a historical context. The basic conviction of the Greeks was that truth was changeless and hence not tied to events. The earliest Christian creeds, such as the Apostles Creed, were composed to counter such views, which tended to overspiritualize Jesus and detach Christianity from history.

---

8. McGrath, *Christian Theology*, 339–42.

In this study our concern is to focus on the here-and-now, on our "this-worldly" tasks and journey and not on the afterlife or on how to get to heaven. That concern, in my estimation, is peripheral to Christianity and serves as a distraction from the urgent "religious" tasks at hand.

Summary

Religion is indispensable in providing guidance and meaning to society. As popularly defined, religion is a means whereby humans interact with the sacred. Such an approach, while valued, is inadequate, for it is prone to dualistic thinking, which distorts religion and reality. In antiquity, religion was a way of respecting all powers that govern one's destiny. Religion was not intended to divide people sociologically but rather to unify society. Religion should be understood as a phenomenon pervading society and not as a distinct element separate from other elements of society. The following definition guides our study: "Religion is human transformation in response to perceived ultimacy." This definition views the role of religion to be dynamic rather than static and radically this-worldly in scope and orientation.

For Discussion and Reflection

1. Define "dualistic thinking," and in a few sentences assess its attractiveness to religious individuals as well as its disadvantage as a way of viewing reality.
2. In your estimation, how helpful is Esposito's distinction between speaking of religion as noun or as adjective? Which approach do you favor? Why?
3. Based on the etymology of the term "religion," which of the three derivations do you find most helpful? Support your answer.
4. In light of the textual discussion of the three etymological derivations of the term "religion," take a few moments to answer the following questions:
    a. What do I hold sacred in my life? How do I show respect for the sacred in my life?

b. What do I consider to be "ultimate" in the universe in terms of power and reverence? How can I find harmony with this power?

c. Am I living thoughtfully and mindfully? How do I fall short of that mark? How can I live more intentionally? Am I lacking in discipline or devotion?

5. Evaluate William A. Young's definition of religion given in this chapter: "Religion is human transformation in response to perceived ultimacy."

6. Go online and learn more about Paul Tillich's definition of religion as that which is of "ultimate concern"? What are the merits and disadvantages of Tillich's view? Do you find his understanding of ultimacy to be too general and impersonal, or do you find it significant precisely because of its breadth and depth?

7. How does the biblical story of Abraham inform and impact your journey of faith? In your estimation, is the doctrine of "election" valid for twenty-first-century Christians?

8. In his discussion of sin and salvation, Alistair McGrath posits various answers to the questions: "From what are we saved"? or "For what are we saved"? Which of his answers do you find most valid? Why?

Chapter 3

The Promise of Nature

Central Idea: Recent scientific developments encourage thinking of the cosmos as an unfolding story, making it possible to assimilate the scientific story of the universe with the narrative pattern that has always shaped religious consciousness.

Key Biblical Passages: Matthew 5:48; Luke 6:36; Romans 8:19–21

IN 1930 THE FAMOUS British physicist James Jeans wrote that modern science paints a distressing picture of a universe hostile to life and consciousness, one destined for death at the hands of entropy. Entropy, as he understood it, indicated that the universe was either indifferent or hostile to life, for all human aspirations were but doomed to final frustration.

Prominent scientists such as Carl Sagan, E. O. Wilson, and Stephen Jay Gould, agree with Jeans, viewing any notion of purpose in the universe to be archaic and illusory. They view all versions of teleology in the universe as psychological projections of human longings for significance onto a universe that is itself devoid of any ultimate purpose. Their disdain for cosmic teleology is particularly evident in their discussions of evolution, which they consider to be absolutely opposed to any vision of cosmic purpose and, therefore, incompatible with religion.

No question in science and religion is more to the point, or strikes more directly at the heart of human concerns, than that of cosmic purpose. And if the universe holds no purpose overall, what does this say about who we are and about what sort of individual destiny awaits us?

The Promise of Nature

Scientific developments during the past century and a half—including the results of evolutionary biology, particle and relativity physics, astronomy and Big Bang physics, and chaos theory (the fact of a self-organizing universe)—now make it possible for us to think of the cosmos as an unfolding story. And since it is in the form of story that religions have always expressed meaning, it is not inconceivable that we can assimilate the scientific story of the universe to the narrative pattern that has always shaped our religious consciousness. In particular, the major ingredients of the new cosmology can be meaningfully contextualized by the story of promise and hope through which Abrahamic religious tradition has already shaped our way of looking at the world.

Until recently science has been somewhat abstract and law-oriented. It has not taken into account the story underlying the laws. And as long as the universe was seen as essentially storyless—as unoriginated, eternal, and necessary—it was not difficult for science to think of nature as pointless. Nowadays, however, much of that thought has changed. The laws of nature are no longer viewed as the offspring of an underlying eternal necessity but as the contingent outcome of a definite story with a definite past. We do not yet know all there is to know about the origin of the cosmos, for example, but at least we can say that it is no longer completely lost in the fog of an eternally remote past. Although we cannot absolutely rule out the possibility that there could have been "many worlds" prior to this one, it is sufficient for our purposes to begin with the singularity of the Big Bang; this gives our universe a relatively clear point of origin.

If, then, the cosmos has a finite past, its evolutionary unfolding can be expressed in a narrative form. And if the cosmos is fundamentally a story, then it is inevitable that we think about the "point" of it all. As we humans question the purpose of our existence, it is proper to think of our purpose in the larger scheme of things. Although we do not expect our search to terminate in any clear conclusion about the larger "point" of the universe story, science has recently brought to our attention some surprising ways in which the cosmic story corresponds with the basic religious sense of reality as rooted in a promise that invites from us the response of hope.

Nature, it seems, can be viewed as having always been pregnant with promise. From the first moments of the cosmic dawn, for example, the physical organization of matter already fell within the almost unimaginably narrow range of numerical possibilities that would allow it to become hydrogen atoms, galactic clusters, supernovas, carbon, life, and eventually minds. The various episodes in this amazing story all developed in ways that could never have been anticipated. Science confesses that it could never have predicted such outcomes at the time of cosmic beginnings. And who knows what outcomes may yet be found within the billions of years of evolution that probably lie ahead.

According to John Haught, longtime professor of theology at Georgetown University and a leading contributor to the science and religion dialogue, even entropy is now being given a new reading. "Instead of signaling only the heat death of the universe, entropy is now positively embraced as an essential condition for matter to realize new possibilities. For without an entropic cosmic tendency toward disassembling or fragmentation, the most primitive forms of order would have dominated indefinitely, keeping the world stuck in an inflexible sameness from age to age."[1] Without entropy, he adds, "matter could not realize its promise. Entropy guarantees that the cosmic story will avoid repeating forever the same refrains, and permits it to wend its way toward an always open and often surprising experimentation with novelty. It is such openness to an indeterminate future that the new scientific accounts of the universe are now setting before us. A theology that makes contact with this cosmic openness will be immeasurably enriched."[2]

The preceding quote surely reminds us of Paul's vision for the cosmos in Romans 8:19–21: "For the creation waits with eager longing for the revealing of the children of God; for the creation was subjected to futility, not of its own will but by the will of the one who subjected it, in hope that the creation itself will be set free from its bondage to decay and will obtain the freedom of the glory of the children of God."

The cosmic future seems more open today than it has at any time since the birth of modern science. A promissory universe, then, such as we have sketched, makes room once again in a scientific age for religious faith. The universe that science is now laying before us, with its openness to new forms of order—such as we see in atoms, cells, brains, and societies—seems truly open to teleological interpretation.

Evolutionary biology is only one level of a whole hierarchy of explanations needed to understand in depth the story of life. Theology can be part of such a hierarchy of explanations. Indeed I think we must at some point appeal to theology to explain ultimately why there is any order or design

---

1. Haught, *Science and Religion*, 178.
2. Ibid.

in nature at all—as well as why there is also instability and process. We can explain life and its complex designs on many levels without opposing one level to the other. Physics, for example, can explain order and design quite adequately from a thermodynamic point of view without interfering with biological accounts. Chemistry too can explain life at its own level. And so can theology. Problems arise only when experts on one level claim that theirs is the sole adequate explanation of life.

Darwin, along with many of his followers, concluded that the theory of evolution undermines the time-honored belief that the order or "design" in living organisms requires a divine designer. And so, if God is thought of primarily as an intelligent designer, evolution does appear to challenge religious belief. However, if God is thought of not simply as the ultimate source of order (or design), but also as the source of novelty (as the biblical God "who makes all things new"), then evolution is consonant with biblical faith in the God of new creation.

A good place to start in understanding the promissory nature of the universe is with the Augustinian suggestion that a creator has richly endowed the universe, from its opening moments, with the potential for evolving toward the kind of complexity we see in the cell and genetic DNA. The sprouting of life and mind in the universe is analogous to the blossoming of an oak tree from the inauspicious beginnings of a simple acorn.

From this starting premise, we move to a second possibility, that God "seeds" the universe with the promise of novelty and a complexity that eventually becomes alive and conscious, at least here on earth, but quite possibly elsewhere in the universe as well. The "word of God," which according to Genesis hovers over creation in the beginning, is a word of promise. The self-organizing universe, inseparable from God's promise of a future, may be seen as continuously moving through a "field of promise," consisting of all the possibilities offered at the start. In some sense God (or "the Spirit of God") is this field of promise.

The idea of "design" is too brittle to represent the richness, subtlety, and depth of the life-process and its raw openness to the future. Life is more than "order." Life requires the continual admittance of disruptive "novelty," and so the idea of "promise" serves suitably to indicate life's and the universe's inherent meaning. This way of "reading" evolution seems consistent both with science but also with religious hope.

The key point is that evolutionary biology, now supported and widened by cosmology, has made us realize that we live in an unfinished universe. Scientific and religious systems, together with living species and all of the cosmos, are part of a process still coming into being. The history of religion, like that of science, is a long series of partially successful but mostly inadequate human attempts to adapt to the inexhaustible depths of the cosmos (which, in part, we label "God"). Religion tries to adapt humans to the world's depth through various symbols, myths, and creeds. But the infinite elusiveness of this depth forever evades exhaustive depiction. And so, the religious quest, like that of science, is always frustratingly incomplete. Thus we humans, much more than animals and plants, often feel a sharp sense of dislocation and lack of correspondence to our world because we are made to adapt not just to actuality, but even more to possibility (what we are calling "promise"). We are, in other words, "genetically wired for a world forever open to the future."[3] The fact that the universe is even now perhaps in the early phases of its full emergence helps us understand why, religiously speaking, we remain always somewhat in the dark, why our answers to the biggest of our questions will always be frustratingly opaque, why we must walk by faith as well as by sight, and also why it makes more sense to live with hope than to yield to despair.

The physical universe is a work in progress, and religions, firmly embedded within nature itself, are continuous with this evolutionary responsiveness. This process of adaptation can by definition never reach a static point of completion. Hence the enormous amount of time involved in cosmic, biological, cultural, and religious evolution should come as no surprise, theologically speaking. The universe, understood as an adaptive process, evolves because in the remote reaches of its endless depth there beckons something like a promise (this is akin to what theologians call "providence"). Promise (providence) is not divine manipulation of nature, but is instead a reservoir of possibilities offered to the world throughout its creative spread.

A central issue keeps reoccurring whenever the topic of evolution arises. If, as we have noted, evolution is characterized by the elements of chance, natural selection, and long periods of time, these qualities have led many scientists to conclude that nature is largely unplanned and undirected. In the light of the randomness, impersonality, and cruelty of natural selection, and the fact that life on earth seems to have appeared only gradually over a period that science now estimates to be 3.8 billion years, can we speak meaningfully of purpose in the universe and of a place or

---

3. Haught, *Deeper Than Darwin*, 145.

role of humans in the cosmos? Fortunately, a group of philosophers and theologians, influenced by a version of Christian thought called "process theology," is addressing this issue.

Process theology, a perspective hospitable to the notion of evolution, reflects on God and nature in the light of ideas developed especially by the philosopher Alfred North Whitehead.[4] This great thinker noted that all of nature, and not just life, is in process of becoming. To account for nature's restlessness, he insisted, we must postulate a principle that explains not only the order we observe in nature, but also the novelty that emerges each fresh moment of the world's becoming. The ultimate source of both the order and the novelty in evolution is "God." God, according to process theology, is not interested simply in maintaining the status quo, but is forever attracting the cosmos toward more complex levels of evolution. Wishing a universe continuously open to new creation, God influences the cosmos by holding out before it, at every instant, new ways of becoming itself. God does not force the world into any rigid design, for such coercion would be incompatible with genuine love. Rather, God's power is persuasive. As the source of novelty, therefore, God is also the reason for the breakdown of present order—in the physical, biological, social, religious, and political realms. Chaos, Whitehead says, is the "halfway house" between trivial and more interesting forms of order.

Evolution occurs because God is more interested in adventure than in preserving the status quo. By "adventure," process theology means the cosmic aim toward more intense versions of beauty, where "beauty" means the harmony of contrasts. In other words, God's will for the world is the maximization of beauty. God stimulates the world toward evolution so that deeper modes of beauty, along with beings capable of enjoying it, will come into existence.

To summarize, process theology argues that the God of biblical religion is a God of persuasive love, the source of novelty, and the stimulus to adventure. Unfortunately, Western theology has regularly domesticated this adventurous deity into the orderly, decent, gentlemanly God of the status quo. Evolution is important, then, for helping us recover a richer and more biblical sense of God.

Reflecting on this new understanding of the universe, process theology can see a new meaning in the random occurrences that might otherwise

---

4. The segment on process theology is adapted from Haught, *Responses to 101 Questions*, 135–43.

seem utterly absurd. What evolutionary scientists vaguely refer to as random mutations and unpredictable events in natural history are characteristics we should expect in a universe that is unfinished and open to new creation. Order is important to have an interesting universe, but there must also be room for random events.

For a process to be called purposeful it must be oriented toward the realization of a value. And so, in its aiming toward beauty, traditionally seen as a "transcendental" value, the universe shows itself to be purposeful. Certainly there is more than this to cosmic purpose. But our universe can justifiably be called purposeful if it is oriented, at least in a general way, toward actualizing instances of beauty. And that is precisely the scientific report: ours is a universe of emergent beauty. The renowned physicist Freeman Dyson writes that the universe follows a "principle of maximum diversity," by which he means that the laws and initial conditions of nature "are such as to make the universe as interesting as possible."[5] On the basis of Whitehead's metaphysics we might broaden Dyson's viewpoint, arguing that the point of this evolving universe is to maximize beauty and, along with beauty, the possibility of subjective enjoyment. This is a world that can glorify and give joy to the Creator as well as to its many creatures.

In an evolutionary cosmos, what do the notions of "evil" and "sin" mean? In a static, pre-evolutionary conception of the universe, evil might understandably have been defined as disorder. But in the world-in-the-making, evil also means anything that interferes with the world's ongoing evolution. In an evolving universe, John Haught suggests, there are two forms of evil: (1) the evil of disorder, examples of which are suffering, war, famine, and death, and (2) the evil of monotony. This evil involves "clinging to trivial forms of order" or "refusing to open up to what is fresh and renewing." One form of such evil, he declares, is the human predilection to "break our connections with the diversity that surrounds us as well as with the process that has produced us. Thinking of ourselves as the final end of cosmic creation, we may no longer feel the need to participate as one species among others in a complex earth-community. Or we may shape our civilized and religious lives in such a way as to exclude relevant social and economic diversity and novelty. In other words, we are tempted to the evil of monotony,"[6] which is known by another name: injustice. Whatever else

---

5. Cited by Haught, ibid., 140.
6. Ibid., 141.

we may understand by "sin," in an evolving universe it includes our refusal to participate in the ongoing creation and renewal of the cosmos.

Recapturing the Sacramental Sense of Reality

John Haught argues that when it is wholesome, religion maintains four components: sacramental, mystical, silent, and active. Each of these dimensions suggests a distinct "way" of being religious, he argues, "but religion is most healthy and alive when it blends all four ways harmoniously. And it begins to dissolve into something other than 'religion' whenever any of the four aspects is isolated from contact with its three partners. In the actual world of religious life, such sundering of one aspect from the others is not unusual. But when this splintering occurs, religion rapidly decays into magic, escapism, or obsession with esoteric teachings, or into cynicism, iconoclasm, or vacuous activism."[7] When, on the other hand, religion concretely preserves the four components in a balanced way, it functions in an ecologically supportive way.

Of these, I am fascinated by the sacramental dimension. Religion is sacramental in the sense that it can speak of unspeakable mystery only through the use of symbols, or what theology calls sacraments. A sacrament, in its broadest sense, includes any object, person or event through which religious consciousness is awakened to the presence of sacred mystery. Historically, most of religion's sacraments have been closely related to nature. For example, the luminosity of sunshine, dawn, and dusk; the experience of wind or breath; the purifying power of clean water; the fertility of soil and life—all of these natural phenomena, and many more, have been used by religions to symbolize the way in which ultimate mystery affects us.

Since nature provides many of the fundamental sacraments of human religion, it is easy to see how the conservation of nature is indispensable for the survival of religion. If we lose the environment, we lose God as well. And it is equally true that when religion loses touch with its sacramental origins, it begins to grow indifferent to the natural world. A sacramental vision, Haught reminds us, makes nature transparent to divinity. In this sense it concedes to nature an inherent value without allowing it to become a substitute for God. According to this Christian perspective, nature is worth saving not because it is sacred, but because it is sacramental.

---

7. Haught, *Promise of Nature*, 73–75.

In his seminal work *Original Blessing*, Dominican scholar Matthew Fox calls for a paradigm shift in religious thinking about human origins and the nature and destiny of human beings, from the fall/redemption paradigm to creation spirituality. The reasons for his appeal are compelling, intellectually and spiritually, and they are harmonious with the view of nature as sacramental.

Fox argues that the fall/redemption paradigm, based upon the doctrine of original sin, developed during medieval times and is essentially foreign to Scripture. This tradition, dualistic and patriarchal, considers all nature "fallen" and does not seek God in nature. This tradition does not teach believers about creativity, justice-making, and social transformation, or about the God of play, pleasure, and delight. This tradition has proven unfriendly to artists, prophets, science, and women.

Creation spirituality, on the other hand, begins with original blessing, embodying the biblical emphasis on the goodness of creation. Fall and Redemption theology begins with original sin and ends with redemption. Creation theology begins with original blessing and flows to all subsequent blessings, including those we share with our loved ones and those we affirm in creativity, compassion, birthing, and justice-making; all are prefigured in the grace of creation. Creation spirituality does not ignore sin, but views it differently. Boredom, depression, arrogance, violence, addictive behavior—these occur when we get cut off from the sense of grace and blessing. Original sin is not "original" or primary in time or in biblical theology but derived. Evil is conceived as neither original nor eternal, but rather as something good gone bad.

Hope for humanity and the future of our planet must be based on a proper understanding of the doctrine of creation, one that is not antithetical to science but rather is the subject of the scientist's search, the source of the prophet's vision, and the subject of the mystic's commitment. According to Fox, the universe loves us every day, and the Creator loves us through creation. The following quotation captures his perspective beautifully:

> Creation is the source, the matrix, and the goal of all things—the beginning and the end, the alpha and the omega. Creation is our common parent, when 'our' stands for all things. Creation is the mother of all beings and the father of all beings, the birther and the begetter. It is all-holy; it is awe-filled . . . . Creation is never finished, never satisfied, never bored, never passive. Creation is always newly born, always making new . . . . How can such a drama be jeopardized as it is today? Only because our species, with its

religions, education, moralities, governments, and economics, has lost the sense of creation. When that happens, nothing is holy; nothing seems worth the struggle for justice that is necessary to preserve it. Community dies, and relations no longer exist.[8]

In his writings on creation spirituality, Fox describes spirituality as a way of life characterized by four paths: (1) The Via Positiva: Befriending Creation; (2) The Via Negative: Befriending Darkness; (3) The Via Creativa: Befriending Creativity; and (4) The Via Transformativa: Befriending New Creation. For each path he provides a signpost or commandment (italicized below):

- Via Positiva: *Thou shalt fall in love at least three times a day*. This applies to human beings, to nature in all its magnificence, and also to activities such as music, poetry, and dance. Creation has much to do with falling in love. The first commandment, one of praise, flows from the awe of being alive.

- Via Negativa: *Thou shalt dare the dark*. Every spiritual journey moves from the surface to the depths, and there is no moving from superficiality to depth without entering the dark. "Daring the dark" means entering nothingness and letting it be nothingness while it works its mystery on us. "Daring the dark" also means allowing pain to be pain and learning from it. Being at home in the dark involves relinquishing control—letting go and letting be.

- Via Creativa: *Do not be reluctant to give birth*. Spiritual discipline in the creation tradition is focused on the development of the aesthetic. Beauty, and our role in co-creating it, lies at the heart of the spiritual journey. Such creativity wrestles with the demons and angels in the depths of our psyches, embracing our "shadow" side as well as our visions and dreams. "To give birth" is to enter the Creator's realm. The work of co-creation engages the image of God (*imago dei*) that is in every person, essential for assisting nature and history in carrying on the creativity of the universe.

- Via Transformativa: *Be compassionate, as your Creator is compassionate*. This commandment, the summation of Jesus' ethical teaching (Luke 6:36), corresponds in meaning to Matthew's passage from the Sermon on the Mount, translated "Be perfect, as your heavenly Father

8. Fox, *Creation Spirituality*, 10–11.

is perfect" (Matt. 5:48). A better rendition of Matthew's Greek word *teleios* is: "Be mature" or "Be complete." As Luke's version makes clear, for humans to be perfect or complete is for them to be compassionate to all creatures. In this understanding, compassion is not about the actions that flow from a superior to an inferior, but as a result of our interdependence. True compassion, therefore, involves a deep respect for other cultures and traditions and the willingness to work together in our need for mutual wisdom.

If spirituality can be defined as "meeting with God in history," as Leonardo Boff defined it, and if a new spiritual era is emerging, then a new meeting with God is also upon us, providing a self-disclosure of God that is less warlike, less patriarchal, and more concerned with compassion, justice, celebration, beauty, and creativity.[9]

Such spirituality requires a paradigm shift in traditional Western thought. To implement fully the implications in paradigms shifts, we consider the contributions of Thomas Kuhn in his classic work *The Structure of Scientific Revolutions*, Kuhn offers the following characteristics of paradigm shifts in science:

- They see nature in new ways
- They require a shift of vision
- They require transformation of vision
- They require conversion
- They require a switch in visual gestalt

Like worldviews or visions, paradigms are community issues, not private ones. Kuhn believes reeducation is greatly needed during the period of a paradigm shift. Such shifts require different roles of different persons—indeed they may require an entirely different kind of person.

Summary

Certain prominent scholars view the notion of ultimate purpose in the universe to be archaic and illusory. Their disdain for cosmic teleology is particularly evident in their discussion of evolution, which they consider to be absolutely opposed to any vision of cosmic purpose and, therefore,

---

9. Ibid., 18–23, 31.

incompatible with religion. Surprisingly, science has recently brought to our attention ways in which the cosmic story corresponds with the basic religious sense of reality as rooted in a promise that invites from us the response of hope. Likewise, a group of philosophers and theologians, influenced by a version of Christian thought called "process theology," has recently formulated a perspective particularly hospitable to evolution. Such an approach is enhanced by the contributions of theologian Matthew Fox, who calls for a paradigm shift in religious thinking about human origins and cosmic essence, from the fall-redemption paradigm to "creation spirituality," a theological perspective that emphasizes original blessing and cosmic goodness rather than sin and damnation.

For Discussion and Reflection

1. What is your estimation of James Jeans's assessment of reality? Do we live in a universe hostile to life and consciousness? If the universe holds no promise or overall purpose, what does this say about human identity and destiny?
2. What is your understanding of the doctrine of creation? Is it compatible with the scientific hypothesis of cosmic evolution? Is it possible to be a creationist *and* an evolutionist? If so, explain how such a synthesis might be constructed.
3. One of the traditional arguments for the existence of God is the teleological argument, based on the apparent design or purpose found in nature. The Intelligent Design movement, popular among evangelical Christians today, relies heavily on this ancient argument, but alters it in a subtle way. Assess the merits of this way of thinking about God as Creator.
4. Do you find the notion of "promise" as a way to explain God's presence and involvement with the world to be more scientifically and intellectually attractive than the idea of "design"? Explain your answer.
5. In your own words, state what is meant by "cosmic story." If entropy is a defining aspect of the cosmic story, how can that story be said to contain promise? Explain your answer.

6. Assess the merits of "process theology." Go online or to a library for additional information or to broaden your understanding of this movement or perspective.

7. Describe the value of viewing nature sacramentally.

8. What is meant by "original sin"? Given the biblical emphasis on the original goodness of the created order (see Genesis 1), is it possible for human nature to change from essentially good to essentially corrupt (fallen or sinful)? Explain your answer.

Chapter 4

The Promise of the World's Religions

Central Idea: Despite disagreements in beliefs and practices among the teachings of the world's religions, and despite the misuse of religion by individuals, groups, and nations, religion's role throughout history is indispensable, providing meaning, hope, and vision to countless generations throughout human history.

Key Biblical Passages: Acts 17:16–36; Ephesians 4:15; 1 Peter 3:9–16

WE LIVE IN A time of skepticism and unbelief, when many voices speak disparagingly of religion. Some of the criticism is deserved, particularly where superstition and abuse abound. But much of the criticism, such as claims that all religions are violent, irrational, intolerant, and deterrents to human progress, is biased, hateful, and erroneous.

Any religion that has lasting power contributes positively to life both personally and socially. Personal devotion provides *ardour*, that is, private piety, but if ardour were the only benefit, it would lead to social chaos, for there would be no common vision. The other side, social discipline, provides *order*, that is, authority and organization, but if order were the only benefit, society would remain static and stagnant, resistant to growth or significant change. The task of religion has always been, and continues to be, twofold: promoting social cohesion and individual identity. Religion promotes the social good by helping human beings live creatively, peacefully, and even joyously with realities for which there are no easy explanations.[1] At its best, religion does so by providing:

1. Armstrong, *Case for God*, 318.

- A coherent framework, perspective, or worldview that provides answers to identity-forming questions such as "Who am I?" "Where did I come from?" "What is the purpose of life?" and "Where will I go when I die?"
- Teachings, rituals, and disciplines directed toward moral or ethical improvement
- Paradigms that guide one's behavior in relationship toward others, oneself, and the sacred
- Consolation and hope in times of calamity, suffering, and death
- Skillful means that teaches human beings how to live fully and compassionately, discovering new capacities of mind and heart

Teaching world religions and global spirituality to college students over a forty-year span, I uncovered numerous parallels between Christianity and other religions, including beliefs, practices, and historical development. This discovery convinced me that if it is true that there is only one God, as monotheism teaches, then every culture and religion contains perspectives and truths that, taken together, not only complement one another but have a revelatory and therefore a promissory nature for the wellbeing of our planet and for every living creature. If "God so loved the world," as the Christian Scriptures proclaim, and if this God is acknowledged as Creator of all, then wouldn't this God love every country and race equally? And if that were true, wouldn't such a God choose to speak through all the world's scriptures simultaneously, thereby manifesting love for all?

The Contributions of the World's Religions: Seven Dimensions

Ninian Smart, the renowned expert in religious studies, devised a model consisting of seven dimensions to speak of the contributions of the world's religions:

- The experiential and emotional dimension
- The mythic and narrative dimension
- The ritual dimension
- The doctrinal and philosophical dimension

- The ethical and legal dimension
- The social dimension
- The material dimension

The Experiential Dimension

Since the sacred dimension of reality is the source of ultimate value, the deepest need of human life is to have an ongoing relationship with the sacred. No matter how religious or non-religious a person might be, at some time everyone experiences the religious impulse, whether it be a need to find meaning in tragedy or a way to express thankfulness for a joyous or transformative event.

All humans experience major life events, such as birth, death, adulthood, and marriage. Such events, known as rites of passage, generate "boundary questions," that is, questions concerning identity, relationship, meaning, and purpose. Religions provide answers to boundary questions experienced during rites of passage. Since all human beings go through rites of passage and wrestle with their identity questions, religious activity is pervasive in human experience.

The Mythic Dimension

In the field of religious studies there are two kinds of truths: *literal truth* (natural, factual, or scientific in nature) and *mythological truth* (religious or symbolic in nature).[2] Religious myths are not fables but rather sacred stories that hold sacred truths within the worldview of a believer. These stories are often recorded in sacred texts but sometimes in oral tradition. They set forth fundamental knowledge regarding the nature of things and the proper way to live. In religion, myths provide answers to boundary questions. They may not be provable historically or logically, but nevertheless they are real in that they guide the behavior of believers.

Myths, based on stories of great religious leaders like Abraham, the Buddha, Jesus, or Muhammad, provide models that guide human behavior within a given faith community and that are important links between belief, believer, and behavior.

---

2. I am indebted to my colleague Walt Weaver, longtime teacher of courses on world religions and world mythology, for bringing this distinction to my attention.

The Ritual Dimension

Ritual is what believers do. Rituals provide believers with a symbolic mode of communication designed to propel them out of ordinary experience and into extraordinary realities.

Taken together, the experiential, mythic, and ritual dimensions constitute what might be called an inward turning force in religions, whereas the doctrinal and ethical dimensions turn outward, ultimately impacting the social dimension.

The Doctrinal Dimension

If rituals are what believers do, doctrines are what people believe. As belief systems, doctrines provide specific answers to boundary questions. Doctrines include creeds or other teaching that attempt to make sense about salvation, destiny, and the nature of the world. While religion is more than simply a set of answers, religious doctrines have a profound effect on the behavior of believers within a religious community. Religious doctrines give focus and order to the symbolic and the mythical.

The Ethical Dimension

Doctrines are foundations to ethics; as people believe, so they behave. Ethics are the key to values and behavior in any worldview, providing the link between beliefs and right action. The Ten Commandments in Hebrew scripture, the Beatitudes or Golden Rule in Christian Scripture, the Five Pillars in Islam, and the Eightfold Path in Buddhism are classic examples of the ethical dimension.

The ethical dimension, religious or secular, provides human beings with guidelines for proper patterns of action. Whether expressed as laws, moral commandments, custom, or a system of values, the ethical dimension is relational, guiding practitioners toward proper relationship with God, each other, nature, and culture. Ethics provide a sense of obligation and responsibility but also mechanisms for bringing harmony and reconciliation when there is a breakdown in ideal relational patterns.

The Social Dimension

The power of belief and behavior comes alive in the social dimension. Without this dimension, religion would be purely private and even aberrational. It is the communal aspect of religion that empowers individuals and results in hierarchical forms of leadership.

The Material Dimension

This dimension includes the physical forms in which a religion is embodied, including structures of worship, sacred art, ritual objects and substances, and extends to natural places and sacred landmarks such as mountains, rivers, trees, sacred cities, and pilgrimage sites.

Contributions of the World's Religions in Comparative Context

The following chart illustrates the promise of the world's religions by examining the positive contributions of eleven religions. Four categories are included for each religion:

1. A core concept or point of entry
2. Perspective on God/the divine/the ultimate
3. View of the human task, goal, or approach to life ("skillful means")
4. View of the individual's destiny/afterlife

Religion	Entry Point	The Divine	Human Task	Human Destiny
Bahai	Social justice and equality: all religions teach the same truth	One God, who has revealed himself progressively through major world religions	To work for social justice and equality; to develop spiritually and draw closer to God	The soul is eternal and essentially good. At death, the soul separates from the body and begins a journey toward or away from God. Heaven and hell are states of being
Buddhism (Theravada)	Reincarnation; nirvana; the Middle Way between extreme asceticism and sensuality	No gods in original Buddhism; Mahayana Buddhists are polytheistic	Practice mindfulness through meditation; to live non-dogmatically through non-striving and non-attachment (Noble Eightfold Path)	Reincarnation until nirvana

Christianity	Human sinfulness and divine salvation; the incarnation, death, and resurrection of Jesus Christ	The Trinity: God as three persons yet as one; God as Creator, Savior, and Judge; Jesus Christ as human and divine	Importance of faith and practice, as revealed through the Bible; necessity of worship and sacraments; to live ethically by loving God, neighbor, and self	Rewards and punishments in heaven and hell
Confucianism	Centrality of society; social cohesion	Not addressed; role of ancestors, who comprise Tian (Heaven)	To fulfill one's role in society with propriety, honor, and loyalty	Not addressed; veneration of ancestors
Daoism (Taoism)	The Dao/Tao (the orderly way or "flow" of the natural world); yin and yang	The Dao/Tao pervades all and operates on the basis of balance between yin and yang	To live harmoniously with nature; to achieve inner peace, harmony, and longevity by "going with the flow" (through detachment and non-struggle)	Humans revert to the state of nonbeing, which is the other side of being

Hinduism	*Samsara* (humans are in bondage to ignorance and illusion); reincarnation	One supreme reality (*Brahman*), manifested in infinite ways	To achieve freedom from *karma* through one's duties (*dharma*); multiple paths (*yogas*) to *moksha* (release/salvation)	Reincarnation until *moksha* (release from the karmic cycle of life on earth)
Islam	Literal inspiration of the Quran; Muhammad as final prophet of God (Allah); the *Ummah* (the superiority of Islamic society)	Strict monotheism; God as powerful yet unknowable; God's will determines all things	Surrender to the will of Allah through the Five Pillars and Sharia Law	The Day of Judgment; Paradise or Hell
Jainism	Avoid bad karma by non-harming living things	The universe is eternal; belief in many deities	To practice austerity and self-denial through Five Vows (non-violence, truth, celibacy, non-stealing, and non-attachment)	Reincarnation until nirvana

Judaism	Covenant of God with Israel (election and promise)	Strict monotheism; God as Creator and Sovereign Lawgiver	To live ethically; centrality of law and ritual; to live life fully	Focus more on this life than on afterlife; beliefs vary from no afterlife to shadowy existence in *sheol* to earthly paradise in the Kingdom of God
Shinto	Purity and purification rituals	Recognize no one god but rather the existence of *kami* (ancient gods and spirits)	Rituals and ceremonies replace dogmatic beliefs or ethics; worship deities and practice purification rituals	Death is bad and impure; some humans become *kami* after death
Sikhism	Overcome the self by aligning one's will with the mind of God	One God	To balance work, worship, and charity; to perform services at temple (*gurdwara*); to become a "saint soldier," fighting for the good	Reincarnation until release from karmic existence and merger with God

While the specific perspectives and teachings of the world's religions differ, sometimes greatly, religion's role throughout history is indispensable to the majority of humans who ever lived. Despite its misuse by individuals, groups, and nations, religion stands at the heart of culture, providing meaning, hope, and vision to countless generations throughout human history. Religion fosters care for nature and reverence for life, and enhances community and humanistic behavior through benevolence, artistic expression, cooperative ventures, shared values, and holistic lifestyles. At its best, religion speaks out against social injustice, offering help to the weak and marginalized in society. Whether through behavior, teaching, or scriptures, religion provides answers to boundary questions, promoting social unity and individual identity.

Being a missionary religion, Christianity is often depicted as intolerant and exclusive of other faiths and religions. In their thinking about other faiths, Christians need to ponder Acts 17:16–36. This passage relates Paul's visit to Athens, a religiously pluralistic city much like Western postmodern culture. When we examine in this passage Paul's treatment of other religions, we note several important points:

- Paul knows a great deal about other religions in his culture, quoting Greek religious texts in his brief speech. This tells us that we should be informed about other religions, avoiding making ignorant claims or charges about them;

- Paul engages respectfully with people of other faiths, even affirming aspects of their belief. Whenever possible, we too should find common ground with people of other faiths;

- Paul is candid and forthright about his own faith, speaking unapologetically and positively about Jesus and the Christian worldview. In their conversation with people of other faiths, Christians should focus on Jesus rather than on controversial doctrines, though it is always wise to know the true differences between religions. However, all inter-faith dialogue should be conducted in love (Eph. 4:15; see 1 Peter 3:9–16).

Another important passage for ecumenical relations is Romans 2:14–15, a passage we discuss in chapter 5.

The Promise of the World's Religions

Summary

In a time of skepticism and unbelief, many voices speak disparagingly of religion. While some of the criticism is deserved, the task of religion continues to be twofold: promoting cohesion and individual identity. At its best, religion promotes the common good by helping human beings live creative, peacefully, and even joyously with realities for which there are no easy explanations. If it is true that there is only one God, as monotheism teaches, then it is both possible and probable that such a God would speak through all the world's scriptures. If "God so loved the world," as the Christian Scriptures proclaim, and if this God is acknowledged as Creator of all, then it is altogether likely that this God loves all humans equally. Ninian Smart, the renowned expert in religious studies, devised a model consisting of seven dimensions to speak of the contributions of the world's religions: experiential, mythic, ritual, doctrinal, ethical, social, and material.

For Discussion and Reflection

1. Whether or not you consider yourself to be "religious," in which dimension of life have you been most profoundly impacted by religion, individually or socially?
2. Explain how religion may or may not have contributed to the formation of your identity.
3. Are there any religious rituals or disciplines that you consider to be essential in your life? If so, name them and discuss why they are important to you.
4. Are there any religious beliefs that you consider to be essential in your life? If so, name them and discuss why they are important to you.
5. Historically speaking, which of Ninian Smart's seven dimensions do you consider to be the greatest area of contribution to cultural progress? To human happiness?
6. Is there a religious story or myth that provides you with significant meaning, consolation, or hope? Explain your answer.
7. If you could choose to have been born in another culture or part of the world, or if you could choose to follow another religion than that of your birth, which would you choose? Explain your answer.

8. According to Ephesians 4:15, Christians are to "speak the truth in love." Give examples of how this attitude might be applied by Christians today, locally and globally. In this light, evaluate Paul's approach to other religions in Acts 17:16–36.

Chapter 5

The Cardinal Virtues

Central Idea: Rules are essential to ethical behavior, certainly to order in society, but so are virtues. Ancient Jewish and Christian writers believed that ethical wisdom was related to the order they saw in nature, which they attributed to God.

Key Biblical Passages: John 1:1, 14; 14:6; Romans 2:14–15

FOR MANY PEOPLE, RULES are indispensable in that life would be meaningless and futile without them. Goals may be individual and personal, but for these people, rules have to be objective and apply to everyone. Imagine playing a game of football, chess, or Scrabble, without them.

Other people think that the emphasis on rules is mistaken. What we are really concerned about in ethics, they say, are the qualities that we admire in other people and hope to make a part of our own lives. Rules are important at times, but goals and virtues are what we really care about. While rules may be regarded as objective and permanent, in reality rules are constantly changing. What endure are the qualities of people that are worth honoring and emulating.

Both approaches, of course, have merit, and each, taken by itself, is overly simple. Early Christians were familiar with the Wisdom Literature of the Hebrew Scriptures, especially the books of Proverbs and Ecclesiastes, which they traced back to the time of the kingdom of Israel. But they knew that there were similar traditions, some of them thought to be older, among the peoples and religions of the Roman Empire.

For Christian and Jewish writers, the way the natural world seemed to teach this wisdom for living could not be separated from their conviction that the order of that world is the work of God's creation. Paul explained it in his letter to the Romans this way: "When Gentiles, who do not possess the law, do instinctively what the law requires, these, though not having the law, are a law to themselves. They show that what the law requires is written on their hearts" (Rom. 2:14–15). Eventually, this effort to relate common human wisdom to a more basic order established by God in creation took the form of a fully developed theory of natural law.

Natural law ethics, in which basic rules are known by everyone through life's experiences, is probably the oldest systematic form of Christian ethics. These laws are not natural laws in the sense that modern science speaks of the law of gravity, which controls all of our actions whether we think about it or not. Rather this moral law is said to be natural in the sense that it is part of who we are and of the world in which we live, so that its requirements are inescapable. Natural law does not apply to us because we are citizens of a particular country or believers in a certain religion. It applies to us because we are human.

Ideas about natural law become important when people find that they have to live together in situations where they lack shared goals and shared traditions. The idea that some things are right "by nature" is found already in Aristotle, and it was developed by Stoic philosophers and Roman lawyers to suit the needs of a diverse empire. The Roman orator Cicero (106–43 BC) spoke of a law that functions in all places alike because it is written into the structure of reality. As we noted earlier, in the Middle Ages Thomas Aquinas developed a synthesis of Christian and classical learning that clearly connected the natural law to God's decrees.

C. S. Lewis seems to have had this in mind when he identified universal truths in concepts such as the Tao (the Way) in ancient China and *rita* (divine Law or Truth) in early Hinduism.[1] In Hinduism, *rita* is the principle of natural order which regulates and coordinates the operation of the universe and everything in it. Likewise, the Chinese speak of the Tao as the essence of reality or the Way of the universe. The ancient Jews conceived of Torah as way, truth, and life. The author of the Gospel of John seems to be alluding to this notion of a universal principle of natural order

---

1. Lewis, *Abolition of Man*, 27–29. In an appendix, "Illustrations of the Tao," Lewis examines eight examples of the Natural Law found in legal and religious texts across cultures of antiquity, 95–121.

when he speaks of Jesus as the Logos (the divine Word) in John 1:1, 14 and also as the Way, the Truth, and the Life in 14:6.

While the basics of what we call "natural law" may not change, our understanding and application of them does. As our knowledge of the world grows and our contact with people who have cultures and ideas different from our own becomes more frequent, the ability to rethink what is morally required of us in light of new knowledge and new experience will surely be needed.

In the end, neither goals nor rules alone provide enough guidance to show us how to live a good life. Seen as a whole, a good life seems to require more than goals and rules. To have a good life we need also to understand who we are as persons. And we do this by examining morality through our shared narrative as humans, creating a vocabulary of personal characteristics that we recognize as essential to our moral lives. These characteristics we call virtues. Virtues are the admirable qualities of persons that emerge from an examination of their narratives and that shape their moral lives.

So what is a virtue, and how can we speak about virtue in ways that retain the richness and variety of our individual narratives while still helping us to come to a systematic understanding of the moral life? An early answer was supplied by Aristotle in his *Nichomachean Ethics*. A virtue, Aristotle said, is a pattern of behavior learned through practice, so that it becomes part of the way a person normally tends to act. Having the virtue of kindness, for example, does not mean intellectually knowing how kind persons should act. Rather persons having the virtue of kindness regularly do the kind thing. Indeed, the Greek word for virtue, *arête*, can be used for any sort of excellence.

Aristotle's way of thinking about virtue entered into Christian ethics many centuries later when Thomas Aquinas adopted the Aristotelian account of virtue as the starting point for his own thinking on the subject. Virtue, Aquinas taught, is a *habitus*, a habit that displays excellence in action, something done so naturally that it is practiced without prior thought or intention.

To this understanding of virtue, an important corollary must be mentioned. Virtues such as kindness, patience, and honesty require more than just doing something regularly, or not doing the wrong thing; they also require doing something well. This aspect, sometimes known as the Doctrine of the Mean, states that a virtuous action is one that finds the right middle point between two ways of doing the wrong thing in a situation, one being excessive and the other deficient. Courage, thus, is a virtue that finds the middle point between the excessive readiness to rush into dangerous situations that we call recklessness, and the lack of ability to face challenges that we call timidity or cowardice. Patience finds the middle ground between a hot-tempered insistence on immediate action and a passive acceptance of anything that happens. People who have acquired virtues are not simply following rules. The virtues have become part of their character.[2]

While many virtues are honored by cultures and societies, four virtues were identified by both Christian and classical writers as of special importance: prudence (wisdom), justice (fairness), fortitude (courage), and temperance (moderation). These were called cardinal virtues (drawing on a Latin word *cardo*), meaning that the moral life turned on these four virtues as a door turns on its hinges.

While different circumstances and lifestyles require different virtues, what makes the cardinal virtues important is that they are the virtues that people need to develop in order to live by whatever other virtues are important to them. And whatever virtues seem to be most important in one person's life, they have to be kept in balance with other good characteristics they seek to cultivate. For example, the merchant who practices only boldness and never patience is not likely to survive very long. The same holds true for most occupations and careers. The idea of the cardinal virtues rests on the insight that we have to acquire some habits in the way we live out our virtues in order to have any virtue work over the long run. Those habits on which the other virtues turn are the cardinal virtues, virtues particularly important to everyone's moral life.[3] The identification of these four may seem somewhat arbitrary, but that is because our modern understanding of what these words means has become rather narrow.[4]

Prudence (wisdom) is tricky to understand in modern terms. We are apt to mistake it for merely being cautious, and we tend to look down on those who seem to be too proper, calling them prudish. We wonder how we can make prudence into a virtue that stands without contradiction alongside courage. Yet it is clear that courage can become mere recklessness without some thought about when it is appropriate to be courageous.

---

2. M. K. "Mahatma" Gandhi, Indian nationalist, spiritual leader, and paragon of moral excellence, often observed that virtue is not like clothing, to be put on, taken off, and changed, but rather something woven into the fabric of one's being.

3. See appendix A for a list of virtues associated with the cardinal virtues.

4. This segment on the cardinal virtues is adapted from Lovin, *Christian Ethics*, 68–73.

Patience, likewise, may become procrastination if we are unable to determine when the time for action has come. Generosity can be merely wasteful if giving is not directed toward real needs in ways that show some prospect for solving the problem. Prudence is a habit of choosing actions that will make other virtues effective.

Prudence means practical common sense, thinking wisely about what one is doing and about the likely results. The wise person seems to know when to act and when to seek more information. A prudent person gives generously, but not blindly. A prudent person cares for people in need but avoids making them dependent on the care of others. Wise people have figured out how to live good lives now.

Thomas Aquinas ranked prudence as the first cardinal virtue because it was concerned with the intellect, which, following Aristotelian practice, has priority over the will. He defined prudence as "right reason applied to practice." It is the virtue that allows us to judge correctly what is right and what is wrong in any given situation. Because it is easy to fall into error, prudence requires us to seek the counsel of others, particularly those we know to be sound judges of morality. Disregarding the advice or warnings of those whose judgment does not coincide with ours is a sign of imprudence.

Justice, like prudence, is a habit of thinking about situations and choices in ways that make it more likely we will actually achieve the good things we intend when we make a moral choice. The distinction between prudence and justice is sometimes difficult to make, but in general, prudence is about the effective pursuit of a particular good, while justice is about the appropriate choice of which goods and goals to pursue. Justice (fairness) includes honesty, faithfulness, and keeping promises.

Justice derives its meaning as a virtue from its primary meaning as the appropriate distribution of things in a society or an institution. A society is said to be just when the things that make it possible for people to have good lives are distributed fairly. Additionally, a just society must assure that persons are treated fairly, including systems to restore justice when it is disrupted.

Justice as a virtue of persons has to do with balancing a wide variety of possible goods to choose the ones that are appropriate. Just persons lead a balanced life between their own needs and the claims of their neighbors, and between the various good possibilities that make claims on their time, energy, and skill.

Justice, according to Aquinas, is the second cardinal virtue because it is concerned with the will. Justice has been defined as the determination to give everyone his or her rightful due. We say that "justice is blind" because it should not matter what we think of a particular person. If we owe a debt, we must repay what we owe. Justice is connected to the idea of rights. Injustice occurs when we as individuals or by law deprive someone of that which he or she is owed.

The third cardinal virtue, according to Aquinas, is *fortitude* (courage). Fortitude is perhaps the most familiar of the cardinal virtues. Fortitude helps us to be bold in the attainment of good and helps us overcome fear and despair. It is the spiritual bravery we need to help us act properly in difficult situations, persevering in the attainment of what we perceive as the good. It can be dramatic, as when rescuers place their lives at risk or when unarmed protestors face down troops and tanks to secure freedom for themselves and others. We also see fortitude in people who face serious illness and death without losing their capacity to care about others or their concern for the future. We recognize fortitude in leaders who risk unpopularity to stand up for principles, or in people who live with dignity in the face of prejudice and discrimination.

While this virtue is commonly called courage, it is different from what we ordinarily think of as courage today. Fortitude allows us to remain steady in the face of obstacles, but it is always reasoned and reasonable. The virtue of fortitude is not the specific acts of daring or self-sacrifice that we admire, but the habit that shapes our choice to act courageously. Prudence and justice are the virtues through which we decide what needs to be done; fortitude gives us the strength to do it.

In fortitude we see most readily how the moral virtues work. It takes discipline to act courageously, a discipline that is built up over a lifetime of taking courage in small things. It takes courage for an awkward fourth grader to face the teasing of classmates or for an office worker to resist the petty humiliations imposed by an abusive boss. Unless we learn to practice such disciplines, it is unlikely that we will be ready to respond when the occasion calls for a sudden act of great risk or for steady endurance in the face of overwhelming danger. What makes fortitude a cardinal virtue is that we cannot act on any of the virtues for very long without it.

Temperance (moderation), like prudence, is also easily misunderstood today. It is often reduced to the concept of abstinence, especially from alcohol. But the virtue of temperance is more than abstinence. Temperance is as much about how we use our minds as it is about how we care for our bodies. Temperance involves knowing what our physical and mental health requires and regulating our pursuit of goals and the things we desire so that everything we do contributes to our long-term wellbeing. Temperance involves knowing our limits and enjoying each good thing in a way that enables us to enjoy other good things in the future. The temperate person knows how to change and grow spiritually, always remaining open to explore new possibilities. Temperate people participate fully in the opportunities and experiences that are available now, but in ways that keep them available for new experiences and for the needs of others in the future.

Temperance, Aquinas declared, is the fourth and final cardinal virtue. While fortitude is concerned with the restraint of fear so that we can act, temperance is the restraint of our desires or passions. Food, drink, and sex are all necessary for our survival, individually and as a species, yet a disordered desire for any of these goods can have disastrous consequences, physical and moral. Temperance is the virtue that attempts to keep us from excess. Temperance is the "golden mean" that helps keep our passion from ruling over reason. The idea is to avoid excessive behavior so that such acts do not dominate or distract from what will make us ultimately happiest.

We have addressed the natural virtues before the supernatural virtues for a reason. The natural leads to the spiritual, but the spiritual arises out of the physical. This principle is basic to all spirituality, for healthy spirituality is holistic. Bodily health, mental health, and emotional health are not peripheral to spirituality; rather, they are the lifeblood of soulwork. As body is to mind, mind to soul, and soul to Spirit, so the natural is prerequisite to the supernatural.

Summary

Ancient people around the globe observed a basic order in the natural world that seemed to teach humans how to live wisely. This system, called natural law ethics, is probably the oldest systematic form of Christian ethics. The moral law was said to be natural in that it is known to everyone, so that its requirements are inescapable. The idea that some things are right "by nature" is found in the Western world as early as the writings of Aristotle. In the Middle Ages the philosopher Thomas Aquinas adopted Aristotle's way of thinking about virtue, stating that a virtuous action is one that finds the right middle point between two extremes, one being excessive and the other deficient. While many virtues are honored by cultures and societies, four virtues were identified by both classical and Christian writers as "cardinal," meaning of special importance: prudence (wisdom), justice (fairness), fortitude (courage), and temperance (moderation).

For Discussion and Reflection

1. This chapter discusses the value of rules, goals, and virtues. How do these differ? Give an example of a rule, a goal, and a virtue. In your estimation, which of these comes first in terms of priority? Does the order differ in priority depending on whether you are thinking of their role individually or for society?

2. When you think of the ethical rules or behavioral values in your life, do you see them as originating with God, in nature, or in society? Explain your answer.

3. Do you consider certain ethical norms universal in application, meaning that they are normative for all humans? If so, list your top three natural laws.

4. What commonality do you find in the Chinese Tao, the Hindu *rita*, and the Jewish Torah? Can you think of a Christian counterpart to these?

5. Describe the Doctrine of the Mean. Do you find this principle to be operative in your life? Explain your answer.

6. In your own words, describe "prudence" as an ethical norm. Why did Thomas Aquinas rank it first among the cardinal virtues? How would you rank the cardinal virtues? Explain your answer.

7. How is fortitude different from courage? Give examples of each, either from your own life or from the example of others.

8. Modern individuals exhibit particular problems dealing with addictive behavior. Give specific examples of how temperance can help you to avoid excessive behavior.

Chapter 6

The Theological Virtues: Faith

Central Idea: The supernatural virtues of faith, hope, and love enable us to live life as God intends. The reorientation of life begins with faith because we must trust that there is a reality beyond ourselves in which our goals find fulfillment and where our efforts finally make a difference. Without faith, personal success is the highest form of goodness we can achieve.

Key Biblical Passages: 1 Samuel 16:7; Matthew 6:25–34; Mark 9:23–25; 11:22–23; Luke 10:29–37; Romans 12:2; 1 Corinthians 13; 2 Corinthians 12:9; Galatians 5:1, 6, 22–23; Philippians 2:2–5; Hebrews 11:1, 6

While Christians agree with the Western philosophic tradition on the importance of virtue, and of the four virtues in particular, they disagree with non-Christian philosophy in their understanding of how the moral life starts and on the severity of the obstacles. There seems to be an impediment at work in our lives that draws us away from the habits of virtue and makes it difficult to act on them. What stands between us and virtue is sin. Sin is much more serious than the simple fact that we often fail to do the things we know we ought to do. Sin is spiritual nearsightedness, a constriction at the center of human life that keeps us turned in upon ourselves, so that we cannot live as God intends. The good news that Christianity proclaims is that God has provided the resources to overcome our moral myopia, expanding our vision by showing us in Jesus what life is like when it is lived in love for God and for other people.

In addition to the moral virtues, there must be characteristic changes in human life that mark the turn from self to God, from limited human resources to divine resources; and these, according to Christianity, are God's gifts, not human achievements. In addition to those cardinal virtues that enable us to learn and maintain the other moral virtues, there must be supernatural virtues, "habits of choice and action that guide us in seeing our lives in relation to God and help us to persevere in that orientation, even when it is not immediately supported by our experience or by people around us."[1]

For Christian writers like Thomas Aquinas, the supernatural virtues were conveniently summarized in the three abiding realities mentioned in 1 Corinthians 13: faith, hope, and love. Like the cardinal virtues, the theological virtues are "hinges" on which the good life turns. Without them all other virtues are unsteady. Without faith, hope, and love, patience and kindness are apt to wilt under stress or, worse, be transformed into manipulative ways to serve oneself under the guise of helping others. Temperance, courage, prudence, and justice make us more effective in the application of moral virtues, but not if our pursuit of goodness is directed, in the end, toward our own gain. What Christian morality requires is a reorientation of our life whereby the theological virtues become central to how we live and to how we relate with other people, and not simply instrumental to our own self-improvement.

Speaking theologically, every power we have is given by God. Like other spiritual qualities, the theological virtues are paradoxical in that they are *gifts* that cannot be obtained by merely wishing for them, but they are also *virtues* that can be cultivated. While their potential is available to all persons alike, the capacity for faith, hope, and love varies with one's constitution and one's social circumstances. Faith is called "the seed," for without it the plant of spiritual life cannot start at all. In fact, so fundamental is faith that none of us can live well for long without it. This is true of all religions, and even the pseudo-religions of modern times such as Socialism, Secularism, and Scientism.

To be effective, four factors go into the transformation process that occurs when supernatural gifts become central in our lives:

1. *Intellectual*: our minds must be renewed. This is what Paul proposed when he exhorted his readers: "Do not be conformed to this world [and its ways of thinking], but be transformed by the renewing of your minds, so

---

1. Lovin, *Christian Ethics*, 76.

that you may discern what is the will of God—what is good and acceptable and perfect" (Rom. 12:2).

2. *Volitional*: our wills must be renewed. All virtues involve the will, and like the other virtues, faith, hope, and love imply a resolute and courageous act of will. This emphasis combines the steadfast resolution that one *will* do something with the self-confidence that one *can* do it. The opposites of this are timidity, cowardice, fear, indecision, and a mean and calculating mentality. Paul exhorts his readers to exhibit this attitude, calling it the "mind of Christ": "Be of the same mind, having the same love, being in full accord and of one mind. Do nothing from selfish ambition or conceit, but in humility regard others as better than yourselves. Let each of you look not to your own interests, but to the interests of others. Let the same mind be in you that was in Christ Jesus" (Phil. 2:2–5).

3. *Emotional*: our hearts must be renewed. In practicing the virtues, our attitude should be serene and lucid, trusting in God and in God's care for us. This is what the first Evangelist, quoting Jesus, exhorts of his followers in the Sermon on the Mount: "Do not worry about your life, what you will eat or what you will drink, or about your body, what you will wear. Is not life more than food, and the body more than clothing? . . . . But strive first for the kingdom of God and his righteousness, and all these things will be given to you as well. So do not worry about tomorrow, for tomorrow will bring worries of its own. Today's trouble is enough for today" (Matt. 6:25, 33–34).

4. *Social*: our priorities and relationships must be renewed. When our state of being is submerged in cares about social circumstances, we become fixated in our own security and wellbeing, trusting in limited resources and relying on others to survive. When our faith turns from the visible and tangible to the invisible and elusive, our priorities become God's, and we become citizens of a different commonwealth, joining in the company of those who find strength out of weakness. As Paul reminds his readers: "[Christ's] grace is sufficient for you, for power is made perfect in weakness" (2 Cor. 12:9). Behind faith, hope, and love stand the resources of the universe. As the author of the letter to the Hebrews famously defines faith: "Faith is the assurance of things hoped for, the conviction of things not seen" (Heb. 11:1). It is with these invisible forces that one must learn to establish satisfactory social relations. In carrying out this task, the theological virtues require a considerable capacity for renunciation.

Faith

Viewed anthropologically, faith is a universal human concern, not necessarily religious in content or context. Faith can be an ordinary part of relationships in general, as in placing trust in someone or confidence in something. Faith helps us get in touch with the dynamic, patterned process by which we find life meaningful. Faith is a way of giving meaning to the forces and relations that make up our lives, how humans see themselves against a background of shared meaning and purpose. Prior to our being religious or irreligious, we are already engaged with putting our lives together and with what makes life worth living, looking for something to love that loves us, something to value that gives us value, something to honor and respect that has the power to sustain our being. These are issues of faith.

Viewed theologically, the reorientation of life to accommodate the centrality of the supernatural virtues begins with faith because we must trust that there is a reality beyond ourselves in which our goals find fulfillment and where our efforts finally make a difference. Without that reality there is no point to worrying about anything except in terms of how it makes our own life better. Without faith, personal success is the highest kind of goodness we can achieve. Without faith, personal success is the highest kind of goodness we can achieve. Religious faith may involve a leap, but such a leap, as physicist (and now Anglican priest) John Polkinghorne reminds us, is a "leap into the light, not the dark."[2] The aim of the religious quest, like that of the scientific quest, is to seek motivated belief about what is actually true. Faith should not be equated with shutting one's eyes or whistling in the dark.

Reasonable faith seeks understanding. Faith is an essential ingredient in making religious claims, but it does not work alone. Theologians use reason, not only to examine the grounds for religious claims, but also to understand them better. Faith may be a distinctive way to gain access to God, but it is not separable from other ways of knowing; in fact, it is a way of knowing. As modern scholarship has identified multiple forms of intelligence, so it recognizes multiple ways of knowing, involving eight human faculties: sense perception, reasoning, emotion, intuition, language, memory, imagination, and—significantly—faith. For some, faith is considered a deterrent to knowledge, because it does not rely on proof. For others, however, faith is the most important way to know, particularly that part of

---

2. John Polkinghorne, *Quarks, Chaos, & Christianity*, 10.

reality that eludes reason or the senses. Surely Blaise Pascal, the celebrated French physicist, mathematician, and philosopher, had faith in mind when he wrote, "The heart has reasons that reason cannot know."

A Biblical Understanding of Faith

For the Bible, faith is the indispensable preliminary, without which true religious experience cannot develop. It involves a person's initial *awareness* of God, but also a continuing attitude of personal *trust* in God. The initiative is with God, but there must be the corresponding movement on the human side, and this is basically what is meant by faith. Religious and moral attainment is impossible without faith. As the New Testament affirms, all things are possible for the one who believes (Mark 9:23). And without faith, "it is impossible to please God (Heb. 11:6).

In the Bible, faith is always relational, the object of faith being God, and the highest personalization is reached in the New Testament proclamation that God is best revealed in the life of Jesus. In this usage faith is a matter of personal relationship rather than abstract knowledge. In the Hebrew Bible the most important of the terms for faith is the root *amen*, meaning to trust someone. To say "Amen" to anyone is to trust that person, and in the Bible, nothing is as sure, permanent, or reliable as God.

Faith is essential to every religious, social, and political perspective, and it stands at the heart of Christianity. The concept is found throughout the New Testament, either as the noun "faith" (*pistis*) or the verb "believe" (*pisteuo*). When we examine the use of these words today, we discover that the common meaning of these words in modern English is very different from their premodern and ancient Christian meanings. When we speak of faith today, we usually have in mind "belief," which we take to mean holding a certain set of "beliefs," that is, "believing" certain doctrines or dogmas to be true. And that modern way of understanding "faith" leads to misreading key biblical texts. For instance, in the Gospels, we often get the impression that Jesus insisted that his followers acknowledge his divine status, almost as a condition of discipleship. Those who beg him for healing are required to have faith before he can work a miracle, and one is commended for calling out: "I believe; help my unbelief" (Mark 9:24–25).

We do not find preoccupation with belief in the other major religious traditions, however, so we wonder, why did Jesus place such an emphasis on it? The answer is that he did not. The Greek word translated as "faith" in the New Testament means "trust, loyalty, or commitment." Jesus was not asking people to "believe" in his divinity, but rather was asking for commitment. He wanted disciples who would engage with his mission to abandon their pride, laying aside their self-importance and sense of entitlement, trusting fully in the God who was their father. In this freedom they were to give what they had to the poor, feed the hungry, and spread the good news of God's Kingdom everywhere, living compassionate lives. Such *pistis* could move mountains and unleash human potential (Mark 11:22–23).

Faith and Belief: Ancient and Modern Meanings

When the New Testament was translated from Greek into Latin by Saint Jerome early in the fifth century, *pistis* became *fides* ("loyalty"). Since *fides* had no verbal form, for *pisteuo* Jerome chose the Latin verb *credo* (from which we get the word "creed"), a word that derived from *cor do*, "I give my heart." In this context, "heart" does not refer primarily to feelings or emotions, though those are involved. Rather, "heart" is a metaphor for the self at its deepest level. When the Bible was translated into English, *credo* and *pisteuo* became "I believe" in the King James Version (1611). But the word "belief" has since changed its meaning. This English word, coming from the Middle English *bileven*, meant "to prize; to value; to hold dear." It was related to the German *belieben* ("to love"), *liebe* ("beloved"), and the Latin *libido*. So "belief" originally meant "loyalty to a person to whom one is bound in promise or duty."[3]

During the late seventeenth century, however, as our concept of knowledge became more theoretical, the word "belief" started to be used to describe an intellectual assent to a hypothetical proposition. Scientists and philosophers were the first to use it in this sense, but in religious contexts the Latin *credere* and the English "belief" both retained their original connotations well into the nineteenth century.

We commonly translate *credo* as "I believe," and we have been taught that saying "I believe" means giving mental assent to the literal truth of each statement in the creed or in the Bible. As we have seen, *credo* does not

---

3. Armstrong, *Case for God*, 87; Fowler, *Stages of Faith*, 11–12. The seminal work on this topic was made by Wilfred Cantwell Smith, a comparative religionist with the linguistic competence to study most of the major religious traditions in the languages of their primary sources. In *Belief and History* and *Faith and Belief*, Smith argues persuasively that the classical writings of the major religious traditions never speak of faith in ways that can be translated by the modern meanings of belief or believing.

mean "I agree to the literal and factual truth of a statement," but rather "I give my heart to," "I commit my loyalty to." Thus, when we say "I believe" at the beginning of the creed, what we are really saying is, "I give my heart to God." And who is this God to whom we commit our allegiance? The rest of the creed tells the story of God as the One known through nature and in Jesus and as present in the Spirit.

The Four Faiths (Four Meanings of Faith)[4]

In the history of Christianity, faith has four primary meanings. The first of these sees faith primarily as a "matter of the head," whereas the remaining three understand faith as a "matter of the heart." Each meaning is described with a Latin term to show its antiquity, as well as how it is understood in English. For each term the opposite is given, for antonyms are often as illuminating as synonyms.

1. Faith as Assent (assensus)

In this first sense faith means simply "belief," which we take to mean holding a certain set of "beliefs," that is, "believing" certain doctrines or dogmas to be true. This understanding of faith as belief is dominant today, both within the church and outside it. Its dominance in modern Western Christianity is due to the Protestant Reformation, which not only emphasized faith, but also produced numerous denominations, each defining itself by what it "believed," that is, by its distinctive doctrines or confessions.

This development also changed the meaning of the word "orthodoxy." Prior to the Protestant Reformation, orthodoxy referred to "right worship," meaning that those who practiced the liturgy correctly were orthodox. Following the Reformation, orthodoxy began to mean "right belief," and faith began to mean "believing the right things."

The birth of modern science and scientific ways of knowing in the Enlightenment also affected the meaning of "faith" and "believe." When Enlightenment thinkers began identifying truth with factuality, that is, as something verifiable, they began calling into question the reliability of the Bible and of many traditional Christian teachings. As a result, "faith" and "belief" came to be contrasted with knowledge and certainty. For skeptics,

---

4. The material in this segment is adapted from Borg, *Heart of Christianity*, 28–41.

faith came to mean "opinion or conviction," something one turned to when knowledge ran out. For believers, faith is what one turned to when beliefs and knowledge conflict.

According to this understanding of faith, the opposite of faith as *assensus* is doubt or disbelief. In its fundamentalist permutation, those who doubt are said to lack faith, whereas those who disbelieve are said to have no faith. While this view is widespread, it puts the emphasis in the wrong place, for it suggests that what God really cares about is the beliefs in our heads, as if having "correct beliefs" is what will save us. A better antonym of faith has been making the rounds lately: the opposite of faith is certainty.

Faith starts with the willingness to recognize and question the core mysteries at the heart of existence: why we exist at all and how to make meaning out of our existence. As a result, it puts on our radar the yearning for the answers to these ultimate questions and the consequent intuition that draws us to the words, ideas, and rituals of the religious tradition that attempts to answer them. We can't know the answers to the ultimate questions like we can know scientific answers, which build bodies of knowledge over time. Religious answers are more like wisdom. With the habit of faith, we are willing to ponder such questions in our hearts and minds. Quoting Augustine, Aquinas says that belief is "giving assent to something one is still thinking about."

We turn now to the meanings of faith that are relational, those having more to do with the heart.

2. Faith as Trust (fiducia)

In its second and higher sense, faith means "trust" in something or someone. In the Bible, it means radical trust in God. Significantly, it does not mean trusting in the truth of a set of statements about God, for that would simply be *assensus* under a different name. While our behavior is important, God seems to be less concerned with our actions than with our character, for our actions flow from our will: "For the Lord does not see as mortals see; they look on the outward appearance, but the Lord looks on the heart" (1 Sam. 16:7).

Faith is like floating in a deep ocean. If you struggle, if you tense up and thrash about, you will eventually sink. But if you relax and trust, you will float. Like the story of Peter walking on the water with Jesus, when he began to be afraid, he began to sink. According to this meaning, the opposite of *fiducia* is not doubt or disbelief, but mistrust, which results in worry and anxiety. Four times in the extended passage from Matthew's Sermon on the Mount, Jesus says to his hearers, "Do not worry," and then adds, "You of little faith" (Matt. 6:25–34). Lack of trust and anxiety go together; if you are anxious, you have little faith.

3. Faith as Faithfulness (fidelitas)

In the Bible, faith is the trustful acceptance of God's promises, particularly of God's desire to bless all peoples and nations of the world. But faith is also trust in God's faithfulness to the promise, that is, in God's ability to deliver Good News to everyone, something that God accomplishes through Jesus Christ and his followers. Because God is steadfast and faithful, we too are called to faithfulness. *Fidelitas* does not mean faithfulness to beliefs about God, whether biblical, creedal, or doctrinal. Rather it refers to radical centering in the God to whom the Bible and creeds and doctrines point.

The English equivalent to *fidelitas* is "fidelity." Faith as fidelity means loyalty, allegiance, the commitment of the self at its deepest level. Its opposite is not doubt or disbelief. Rather, as in human relationships, its opposite is infidelity, being unfaithful to our relationship with God. To use a striking biblical metaphor, the opposite of this meaning of faith is adultery. Another vivid biblical term for infidelity to God is idolatry, meaning not so much the worship of idols as false gods, but centering in something finite rather than the sacred, which is infinite and beyond all images. As the opposite of idolatry, faith means being loyal to God "and not to the seductive would-be lords of our lives," whether one's nation, affluence, achievement, family, or desire.[5]

In the Hebrew Bible, faith as fidelity is the meaning of the first of the Ten Commandments: "You shall have no other gods before me." In the New Testament, it is the meaning of the Great Commandment: "You shall love the Lord your God with all your heart, soul, mind, and strength." This commandment is followed immediately by the exhortation to "love your neighbor as yourself." *Fidelitas* means being faithful to these two great relationships: God and your neighbor. And one's neighbor, as Jesus explains in the parable of the Good Samaritan, is first and foremost the person who is in need of help (Luke 10:29–37).

---

5. Ibid., 33.

One is faithful to God, therefore, by being attentive to these two primary relationships. We are attentive to God through worship, prayer, and practice, and faithful to our neighbor through a life of compassion and justice. To be faithful to God also means to love that which God loves, which includes the whole of creation.

4. Faith as Vision (visio)

As the English word "vision" suggests, faith is a way of seeing reality, and how we view the whole affects how we respond to life. There are basically three ways we can see the whole:

- We can see reality as *hostile and threatening*, and therefore respond to life defensively, doing whatever we can to survive, for that is all that matters. Many forms of popular religion have viewed reality this way: God (or Life, or Nature) is going to get us, unless we behave the right way, practice the correct rituals, offer the right sacrifices, or believe the right things;

- We can see reality as *indifferent* to human purposes and ends. Although this response to life will be less anxious than that of the first way, we are still likely to be defensive and precautionary. We respond by building up whatever security we can, even enjoying and seeking to take care of the world, but ultimately we are likely to be concerned primarily for ourselves and those who are most important to us;

- We can see reality as *life-giving, nourishing, and full of promise*. To use a traditional theological term, to see reality as filled with wonder and beauty, and to nourish and spread this goodness, leads to radical trust. It frees us from the anxiety, self-preoccupation, and concern to protect the self with systems of security that mark the first two viewpoints. It leads to the ability to love and to be present to the moment. It generates a commitment to spend oneself for the sake of a vision that extends beyond ourselves. It leads to a life marked by the natural virtues, or to use Paul's words, it leads to a life marked by the "fruit of the Spirit": love, joy, peace, patience, kindness, generosity, faithfulness, gentleness, and self-control" (Gal. 5:22–23). These qualities are the result of a way of life that Paul characterizes as "freedom" (Gal. 5:1); freedom *from* evil and from allegiance to false authorities; freedom *for* love. For Paul, faith becomes active "through love" (Gal. 5:6).

The Theological Virtues: Faith

To understanding faith as *visio* is to see reality as gracious; its opposite, un-faith, views reality as hostile and indifferent. This meaning of faith is closely related to *fiducia*, to faith as trust. Trust and vision go together; trust in God—the God of promise and faithfulness—and how we view God go together. In this way of life, radical centering in God leads to a deepening trust that transforms the way we view reality and live our lives. Seeing, living, trusting, and centering are all related in complex and salutary ways.

As we have noted, faith is relational, but this does not mean that beliefs don't matter. There are affirmations that are central to the Christian faith, affirmations such as the reality of God, the centrality of Jesus, and the significance of the Bible. These beliefs are essential, not only for Christians, but for people of all faiths, when properly understood. Faith as a way of seeing at the deepest level requires avoiding the human tendency toward excessive precision and certitude. Christian theology has often been plagued by both—the desire to know too much and to know it too precisely. Our minds tell us that such knowledge is not possible—perhaps not even desirable—and people cannot easily give their heart to something that their mind rejects. Properly understood, a deep but humble understanding of Christian faith as *assensus* is close to faith as *visio*. As we have seen, biblical and theological faith need not be viewed as assent to narrow propositions or as fulfilling specific requirements, but as a persuasive and compelling way of seeing reality.

While faith involves the mind, faith is primarily the way of the heart. Given the premodern meaning of "believe," to believe in God is to love God and to love that which God loves. The Christian life is as simple and challenging as that. Faith precedes hope and love because it is willing to paint the canvas of reality wide enough to ask the ultimate questions; hope then follows.

The theological virtues are strengthened and built up by self-discipline, and not by discussing opinions. Intellectual difficulties are by no means the most powerful among their obstacles. Doubts are inevitable, but how one deals with them depends on one's character.

Faith, hope, and love are maintained less by dialectical skill as by the virtues of patience and courage, for we must be willing to wait patiently until we are spiritually mature, however far off that might seem to be. And secondly, we must be willing to take risks. Life nowhere offers one-hundred percent security, and for our convictions least of all. Employed in gaining wealth, a merchant must risk his property. Employed in taking life, a soldier must risk his own life. Employed in rescuing lost souls, ministers must risk their own soul. The stake automatically increases with the prospect of gain.

It is a condition of all learning that one accepts a great deal on trust, that one gives the teacher the benefit of the doubt. Otherwise one can learn nothing, and remains shut out from knowledge. To have faith, hope, and love means to take a deep breath, to tear oneself away from daily cares and concerns, and to turn resolutely to a wider and more abiding reality. We begin with the insights of the past, listening intently to the truths in Scripture.

Summary

In addition to the moral virtues, there must be changes in human life that mark the turn from self to God, from limited human resources to divine resource. And these must be God's gifts, not our achievements. Without faith, hope, and love, natural virtues are apt to evaporate under stress or, worse, to be transformed into attempts to get one's own way under the pretext of consideration for others. Temperance, courage, prudence, and justice make us more effective in the application of moral virtues, but these will not help us very much if our pursuit of goodness is directed, in the end, toward our own gain. What we need is a reorientation of our life so that the theological virtues become central to what we are seeking and relationships with other people are not just instrumental to our own self-improvement. To be effective, four factors go into the transformation process that occurs when supernatural gifts become central in our lives: the renewal of our mind, our will, our heart, and of our priorities and relationships. Faith is essential to every religious, social, and political perspective, and it stands at the heart of Christianity. Christianity expands the human vision by showing us in Jesus what life is like when it is lived in love for God and for other people. In the history of Christianity, faith has four primary meanings; the first of these sees faith primarily as "belief," a "matter of the head," whereas the remaining three understand faith as relational, as a "matter of the heart."

For Discussion and Reflection

1. If, as noted earlier, Christian anthropology begins with original blessing and not original sin, how should we view "sin"? The text speaks of sin as "spiritual nearsightedness" or "moral myopia." Does this understanding

The Theological Virtues: Faith

downplay the role of sin? If so, what metaphor would you use to define sin's role in social and human life? (In this regard, consider consulting the discussion "from what are we saved" in chapter 2).

2. The theological virtues are considered to be "gifts" as well as "virtues." Explain the similarities between these concepts, as well as the key distinction between them.
3. In your own words, explain the role of faith in spiritual transformation.
4. If faith is said to be related to the intellect, what is the first step in the renewal of one's mind?
5. In your own words, explain the meaning of the biblical cry for help: "I believe; help my unbelief" (Mark 9:24–25).
6. Explain how the meaning of the word "belief" has changed since biblical times.
7. While beliefs are said to be secondary in matters of faith, this does not mean that beliefs don't matter. The text mentions three tenets that should be considered central to the Christian faith. Can you think of any additional affirmations you would add to this list?
8. In your estimation, what is the primary insight gained from reading this chapter?

Chapter 7

The Theological Virtues: Hope

Central Idea: The reorientation of our lives, required by faith, also involves hope. Hope is the inseparable companion of faith. Faith gives us a reason to live; hope keeps us alive. Faith gives hope its assurance, but hope gives faith its breadth. In the Christian life, faith has the priority, but hope the primacy. As faith seeks understanding, so also hope.

Key Biblical Passages: Psalm 33:18; 119:116; Jeremiah 14:8; 29:11; Romans 4:15–22; 8:18–25; 11:22; 15:8; 1 Corinthians 13:12–13; 15:2; 2 Corinthians 1:20; 5:5; Galatians 5:5–6; Ephesians 2:12; Colossians 1:27; 1 Thessalonians 1:3; 4:13; 5:8; Hebrews 6:19; 7:19; 11:8–9; 1 Peter 1:3–9, 13–17, 21; Revelation 21:1, 5

THE SUPERNATURAL VIRTUES REQUIRE a fundamental reassessment of our lives. If the natural virtues challenge the mistaken choices we have made and the wrong we have done, the supernatural virtues challenge our ideas about our moral ability. In retrospect, the feeling that we have lived consistently moral lives and that we merit the rewards we have received dissolves before the recognition that we have essentially served our own needs, even at those points where we were apparently concerned for the welfare of others. For that reason the reorientation of life by faith also requires hope.[1]

Despair is often the byproduct of spirituality. Once we begin to measure our lives by the orientation of self toward God that faith requires, any honest assessment of what we can accomplish becomes futile. Without

---

1. Lovin, *Christian Ethics*, 76.

hope of enhanced vision and greater resources, it would be impossible to continue the reorientation of our lives that the supernatural virtues require of us. Hope is the habit of believing that happiness is a possibility and then choosing to act accordingly. It is the habit of embracing a higher standard of behavior because we believe that if we do, we will in fact turn into better, happier versions of ourselves, even if we know we will never be perfect.

Faith and Hope Together

Hope is the inseparable companion of faith, the habit of acting on our faith. John Calvin spoke of hope as faith taken to the next level, calling hope "perseverance in faith." Faith gives us a reason to live; hope keeps us alive. Despair, hope's opposite, robs us of vitality, turning dreams into nightmares, vision into blindness. Faith, the foundation upon which hope rests, nourishes and sustains that faith. Apart from hope, faith becomes fainthearted and ultimately dead. Christian hope is nothing other than the expectation of those things that faith has believed to have been truly promised by God. Thus faith believes God to be true; hope awaits the time when this truth is made manifest. Faith believes that eternal life has been given to us; hope anticipates its manifestation. Faith binds us to Christ; hope opens this faith to the comprehensive future of Christ. In the Christian life "faith has the priority, but hope the primacy."[2] Thus it is that faith gives hope its assurance, but hope gives faith its breadth and its life.

Using an analogy from the physical body, faith and hope work together like our two lungs, or like the two hemispheres of our brain. As a pair of scissors is worthless without both blades working together, so faith and hope, working in tandem, help us actualize our God-given potential.

Believers whose lives and attitudes are characterized by faith and hope are sometimes viewed as naïve, because they trust in that which they cannot see and hope for things that seem unrealistic, or as Pollyannaish, because they always appear positive and upbeat. But my understanding of faith and hope is not limited to happy days or to good times. The only way people grow to be mature in their faith is to face their deepest fears and confront the greatest problems their society and world are facing and not lose hope.

At the beginning of my teaching career I recall confronting my parents with a list of personal fears and doomsday scenarios. My mother responded with the hope that fueled her faith in those times when her life was at risk

---

2. Moltmann, *Theology of Hope*, 20.

as a missionary in Colombia—the Syria and Iraq of its day in the sense of violence, anarchy, and deep sectarian conflict—declaring that "the best is yet to come." My wife Susan, an effective pastoral counselor, asks her clients to name the worst thing that can happen as a result of the situation they are facing. She understands that when persons are willing to confront their deepest fear, that that becomes their first step to victory. Faith and hope are inseparable, but they should never be confused with mere wish-fulfillment. They are most powerful when they are related to problems and threats in the real world.

Hope can sustain us through trials of faith, through human tragedies or difficulties that might seem overwhelming. In such circumstances, hope becomes an "anchor of the soul" (Heb. 6:19). In the words of Pope Benedict XVI: "a distinguishing mark of Christians [is] the fact that they have a future."[3]

Hope

As Jürgen Moltmann reminds us in his book, *Theology of Hope*, when Christians contemplate the concept of hope, they are pondering the doctrine of eschatology, often defined as the "doctrine of last things," meaning speculation concerning the end of the world or what happens when one dies. As we see historically, apocalyptic theories abound during times of uncertainty, suffering, or persecution. At such times people ponder the future, conjuring utopian visions or issuing dire predictions. Unfortunately, the same holds true today, as apocalyptic cults, sects, even caliphates, flourish across the globe.

Whatever the word eschatology conjures in common speech, for Christians eschatology is a "doctrine of hope," for they are encouraged to live and think proleptically, that is, out of the resources of the future, as though the future were now.[4] From first to last, Christianity is hope, forward looking and forward moving, and therefore also positively revolutionizing and transforming the present.

While speaking of the future, Christian eschatology is hopeful about the future, but it does not speak of the future as such. It sets out from a definite reality in history and announces the future of that reality, its future

---

3. Pope Benedict, *Spe Salvi* ("In Hope We Are Saved"), the papal encyclical letter dated November 30, 2007, §2.

4. This concept is explored in the epilogue as "realized eschatology."

possibilities and its power over the future. Christian eschatology speaks of Jesus Christ and his future: Christ is our hope (Col. 1:27). It recognizes the reality of the raising of Jesus and proclaims the future of the risen Lord. In thus announcing Christ's future in terms of promise, Christian eschatology points believers "toward the hope of [Christ's] still outstanding future. Hope's statements of promise anticipate the future. In the promises, the hidden future already announces itself and exerts its influence on the present through the hope it awakens."[5] Hope's statements of promise, therefore, do not result from experience, but are the condition for the possibility of new experiences. They do not seek to illuminate the reality which exists, but the reality that is coming.

Everywhere in the New Testament, the Christian hope is directed toward what is not yet visible: "Now hope that is seen is not hope" (Rom. 8:24). Christian hope is resurrection hope, and it proves its truth in the contradiction of the future prospects it offers and guarantees: righteousness as opposed to sin, life as opposed to death, glory as opposed to suffering, peace as opposed to discord. Instead of portraying God as being wrathful and vengeful, as so many have done throughout history and are doing even today, it is vitally important to present hope as the foundation and the mainspring of theological thinking. That is why Jesus stands at the midpoint of history, reflecting God's true nature and pointing the way to a hopeful future. The question whether all statements about the future are grounded in the person and work of Jesus Christ provides the touchstone by which to distinguish the spirit of eschatology from that of utopia.

A Biblical Understanding of Hope

In English usage the word "hope" covers a wide range of meanings, and this holds true for the Bible as well. In both the Old and the New Testament the word "hope," whether as noun or as verb, points to a range of experience and meaning often missed in casual reading.

In the Hebrew Bible (Old Testament), hope sometimes describes a human condition of security and prosperity, in which individuals fear no threats and are confident that the future will sustain that security. However, in religious contexts, hope is defined not so much by the distinct shape of specific desires and expectations as by the fact that hope springs from God's creative and sustaining power and that it moves toward a good that

---

5. Moltmann, *Theology of Hope*, 17–18.

is congruent with that power. Many images articulate the conviction that God alone provides the source and the object of our trust: God is a rock that cannot be moved, a refuge and fortress that offer ultimate security for the afflicted.

Throughout the Old Testament, God is recognized as the "hope of Israel" (Jer. 14:8). God's steadfast loving-kindness, revealed in repeated deeds of fidelity, gives the people of Israel confidence that God's promises will be fulfilled in the future. Thus God is the basis of all hope (Ps. 33:18). Hope as a living, present bond between the God of hope and the hoping Israel becomes a major definition of the life of the righteous community. The response of the faithful is thus one of trust, through which one commits one's cause to God, holds fast to God, and lives in serenity and peace under God's protection. The confident expectation of future gladness leads to waiting in patience and courage.

False hope, namely hope in anyone or anything other than God, leads to chaos and disaster. Neither weapons of war, nor wealth, not idols can give lasting security. In the face of anticipated destruction, Jeremiah articulates the theme of the new covenant in classic words of hope: "I know the plans I have for you, says the Lord, plans for your welfare and not for harm, to give you a future with hope" (Jer. 29:11).

Hope is a primary term in the New Testament. The word appears only as a noun or verb and never in adjectival or adverbial form, probably because the emphasis is not on subjective feeling (hopeful or hopefully) but on the objective nature of forces determining the human situation. For that reason the noun is never modified, as in "good" or "bad" hopes.

In the New Testament, hope occasionally describes a human expectation concerning the future that accords with a person's desires and expectations, but, as in the Old Testament, the emphasis is one's relationship with God. Here too hope is grounded in God, sustained by God, and directed by God. As such, hope is a reality within which humans may dwell. Hope is simultaneously the response by God's people to divine activity in their presence and on their behalf. If hope is fixed on God, hope embraces at once the three Hebrew elements of (1) expectation of the future, (2) trust, and (3) the patience of waiting. The connection of hope with faith in Hebrews 1:1 ("faith is the assurance of things hoped for") is quite in keeping with the Old Testament association of hoping and believing.

Paul's writings contain the most developed concept of hope in the New Testament. The famous triadic formula of "faith, hope, and love," noted in Paul's "love hymn" in 1 Corinthians 13, is found twice in 1 Thessalonians, Paul's earliest letter (1:3 and 5:8). Similarly, the three virtues are interrelated in Galatians 5:5-6, where hope, as a gift of the Holy Spirit, allows believers to actualize faith through love. In 1 Thessalonians 4:13, Paul warns his readers not to grieve, "as others do who have no hope" (cf. Eph. 2:12), meaning not that they cannot imagine a future after death, but rather that they can have no well-founded trust in it. In 1 Corinthians 13:12-13, hope is not concerned with the realization of a human dream of the future, but with the confidence that waits patiently for God's gift.

Hope is one of the important components in Paul's dynamic understanding of faith. Strong faith and strong hope go together, as Paul indicates, using Abraham as an example in Romans 4:15-22. For Paul, hope emanates from faith, for hope reflects the guarantee that what God has begun in Christ will be brought to consummation (2 Cor. 5:5). Hope is the linkage between what was begun in believers through their baptism and what will be completed at their resurrection (Rom. 11:22; 1 Cor. 15:2).

Romans 8:18-25 is an important text in that it shows that God's plan includes hope for the creation as well, which will share in freedom from decay and "obtain the glorious liberty of the children of God" (8:20).

Hope is a salient word in 1 Peter, which has been called the "letter of hope." In this epistle, hope has a present connotation. It is a "living hope," a mark of rebirth (1:3). The new life is participation in the resurrection of Jesus Christ. It is the eschatological gift that enables us to live as if the future is a present reality; therefore, hope is the power of this life. The source of our faith and the sustainer of our hope is God (1:21). Hope is the issue at stake in religious persecution; hope is to be confessed, defended, and explained on the witness stand. The defense that best conforms to this hope employs gentleness, courage, forgiveness, and reverence (3:13-17). As in Paul, the prime corollaries of hope are faith, joy, and love (1:3-9).

The Four Hopes (Meanings of Hope)

In the history of Christianity, hope has four primary meanings. The first of these describes a merely human condition, whereas the remaining three understand hope biblically and theologically.

1. Hope as Desire (Wish-Fulfillment)

In this first sense, "hope" denotes an expectation concerning the future that usually accords with a person's wishes or desires. As children we all wish for things we do not currently have, sometimes even for things we cannot have, items we have seen in magazines, on television, at a store, or when we visit friends. People ask us what we want for Christmas or for our birthday, and this primes the pump of desire. As we get older, we often wish for a change in relationships or in our circumstances. Whether these desires are realistic or not, hopes that are not firmly grounded often result in disappointment, shame, and sometimes in disaster.

As with faith, we now turn to three meanings that are relational in nature.

2. Hope as Trust

In its second and higher sense, hope means *trust in* something or someone. As with all virtues, it arises from the will, not the passions. Like *fiducia*, faith means radical trust in God or desire for God. Significantly, it does not mean asking God for material things or even for a change of circumstances, for that would simply be wish-fulfillment under a different name. In the Bible, God is the source and ground of hope. This explains why there can be but one hope (Eph. 4:4). Like *fidelitas*, hope is also trust in God's faithfulness to the covenant, that is, in God's promise to bless the patriarchs and through them, the world, something God accomplished through Jesus Christ and his followers. Because God is steadfast and faithful, we too are called to faithfulness. In the Christian tradition, hope in Christ means that the one who hopes has a firm assurance.

3. Hope as Promise

In the Bible, the people of God are called to a life of pilgrimage, mobility, and change, guided by nomadic consciousness. The prototypical model for the journey of faith is found in the patriarchal stories of Genesis 12–50, starting with the story of Abraham, a story summarized in Hebrews 11:8–9: "By faith Abraham obeyed when he was called to set out for a place that he was to receive as an inheritance; and he set out, not knowing where he was going. By faith he stayed for a time in the land he had been promised, as in a foreign land, living in tents, as did Isaac and Jacob, who were heirs with him of the same promise."

Nomadic religion is a religion of promise. The nomad does not live within the cycle of seedtime and harvest, but in the world of migration. Nomadic consciousness influences its adherents socially, economically, politically, but also theologically. The inspiring, guiding, protecting God of nomads differs fundamentally from the gods of the agrarian peoples. The gods of the nations are locally bound. The God of the nomads, however, is not bound territorially. This God journeys with them, leading believers to a future that is not mere repetition and confirmation of the present, but is the goal of the events now taking place. The decision to trust in the call of such a God is a decision pregnant with future. The peculiar thing about the people of Israel is that when they passed from the nomadic life to the settled life of Canaan, they did not abandon their nomadic religious perspective. Rather, they took with them the wilderness perspective, together with the corresponding understanding of existence, a decision that would serve them well into the future, providing unity and identity in their diaspora experiences.

The whole force of promise, and of faith in terms of promise, bound Jews and later Christians to the future. Divine promise, because it emanated from the freedom of God, indicated that the expected future was open to develop in ways not currently envisioned, irrespective of possibilities inherent in the present. In the Bible, the concept of promise creates an interval of tension between the uttering of the promise and its fulfillment. In so doing, the concept of promise provides humanity with the freedom to believe or disbelieve, to obey or disobey, to be hopeful or resigned. If history is connected to the God who promises, then there is no need to construct hard and fast correspondence between promise and fulfillment, or for making predictions or calculations for the future. Rather, the fulfillment may quite likely contain elements of newness and surprise over and against the promise as it was received. If they are God's promises, then God must also be regarded as the subject of their fulfillment. The peculiar character of the biblical promises can be seen in the fact that the promises are not satisfied by the history of Judaism or Christianity, but that on the contrary these experiences of history gave them constantly new and wider interpretation.

Discontentment with God's promise is the root sin in the Bible (see Ps. 106:24), whereas confidence in the promise is the essence of hope (Ps.

119:116). In the Christian tradition, all of God's promises to humanity are affirmed as true in Jesus Christ (2 Cor. 1:20). Through him all who believe become children of Abraham and heirs of God. Through Christ God guarantees the promise to all who share the faith of Abraham (Rom. 4:16), confirming his promises to the patriarchs by bringing Gentiles within the covenant (Rom. 15:8), even those who have been "strangers to the covenants of promise, having no hope and without God in the world" (Eph. 2:12).

4. Hope as Expectation

Like *visio*, hope at its best sees possibilities, because it is related to creativity and imagination. Faith binds humans to Christ; hope sets this faith open to the comprehensive future of Christ. Where faith is rooted in Christ, who was raised from death and the grave, where the bounds that mark the end of human hopes are broken in the raising of the crucified one, there faith can and must expand into hope. There faith's hope becomes a "passion for what is possible," because it can be a passion for what has been made possible.[6]

As we have seen, hope rooted in promise is related to change, not only for individuals or for society but also for a new creation. John of Patmos, visualizing a "new heaven and a new earth" (Rev. 21:1), quotes God as saying: "See, I am making all things new" (Rev. 21:5). Paul, likewise, envisions a new creation in Romans 8:19-21. John Calvin seems to have had this in mind when he writes in his *Institutes*: "Hope is nothing else than the expectation of those things which faith has believed to have been truly promised by God."[7]

In his writings, C. S. Lewis relates hope to human "longing."[8] In *Mere Christianity* he argues that there are all sorts of things in this world that promise satisfaction, but they never quite deliver. "I Can't Get No . . . Satisfaction," sing Mick Jagger and the Rolling Stones, and many people agree, finding in their own lives a deep longing for things that this world cannot

---

6. The phrase in quotation marks is from Kierkegaard; cited in Moltmann, ibid., 20.

7. Cited in Moltmann, ibid.

8. In his autobiography, *Surprised by Joy*, Lewis refers to profound moments of longing as "Joy," by which he meant feelings that point beyond themselves. He is quick to point out that in speaking of joy he is not indulging in nostalgia, which is a longing for the past. Nor does he agree with Freud and other modernists who explain spiritual longings as products of displaced sexual desire.

satisfy. Most of our physical desires are rooted in things that can be met: for hunger there is food, for exhaustion there is sleep, for sexual desire there is sex, for intimacy there is friendship and marriage. But Lewis found within himself a deeper longing, a universal desire that he believed no experience in this world could satisfy, and he used that experience to argue for the existence of an afterlife, maintaining that the most probable explanation was that humans were made for another world. "I must keep alive in myself the desire for my true country," he writes, "which I shall not find till after death; I must never let it get snowed under or turned aside; I must make it the main object of life to press on to that other country and to help others to do the same."[9] Lewis concluded that such thinking is not irresponsible or evasive: "If you read history you will find that the Christians who did most for the present world were just those who thought most of the next . . . . It is since Christians have largely ceased to think of the other world that they have become so ineffective in this. Aim at Heaven and you will get earth 'thrown in'; aim at earth and you will get neither."[10]

Arguably the leading apologist (defender) of Christianity in the twentieth century, Lewis's concept of heaven was highly original, as demonstrated in his theological fantasy *The Great Divorce*. To Lewis's credit, the desire for immortality alone, that is, for heaven as something earned or as reward, is poor justification for becoming a Christian. The essence of Christianity—its highest virtue—is not the negative ideal of unselfishness, abstinence, or self-denial but rather the positive ideal of love. While the Gospels tell us to deny ourselves and to take up our crosses, this is done in order to be like Christ, for as Lewis stresses, those who follow Christ will be with Christ eternally. Heaven, in Lewis's understanding, turns out to be the consummation of earthly discipleship.

In his famous sermon, "The Weight of Glory," Lewis speaks of discipleship as love of one's neighbor. It may be possible, he notes, for a person to think too much of his own potential glory hereafter, but it is hardly possible for him to think too often or too deeply about that of his neighbor. The weight of our neighbor's glory should be laid daily on our back, he adds, for it is a load so heavy that only humility can carry it. For Lewis, there are no ordinary people: "Next to the Blessed Sacrament itself, your neighbor is the

---

9. Lewis, *Mere Christianity*, 120.

10. Ibid., 118. To these options a third alternative needs to be added, the concept of "realized eschatology," discussed in the epilogue below. Although Lewis would not have been familiar with the term, his post-conversion life clearly epitomizes its transformative potential.

holiest object presented to your senses."[11] If our neighbors are Christian, they are holy because in them Christ is truly hidden.

Prior to becoming a Christian, Lewis was skeptical of religion in general, specifically of Christian doctrine. People who knew him as a young man said he was a "prig," in the British parlance. His arrogance was not without reason, for he had a remarkable intellect. As a student at Oxford's University College in the early 1920s, Lewis achieved a rare feat—a "triple first," meaning he was first in his graduating class in all three major subjects: English, philosophy, and classics. In 1926, a year after joining the Oxford faculty, Lewis met J. R. R. Tolkien, later famous as the author of *The Hobbit* and *The Lord of the Rings* trilogy. "No harm in him," Lewis wrote in his diary. "Only needs a smack or so."

But conversion changed C.S. Lewis. The story of his progression from atheism to Christianity is documented in *Surprised by Joy*, his spiritual autobiography. The effect of his conversion was explosive. Prior to his conversion, his literary productivity was slim, limited to two volumes of verse. His conversion gave him a mission and a voice, resulting in a veritable torrent of books, essays, novels, and radio talks, including more than thirty published titles, all with Christian themes. When he became a Christian, his view of human beings changed and his haughtiness was gone. Lewis determined to live a life of humility and charity. As a result, he determined to reply personally to the twenty to thirty letters he received daily from admirers, writing twenty thousand letters over the course of his lifetime. Maintaining this practice consumed hours every day and was especially taxing in his final days, as his health began to fail. His generosity is evident by the size of his estate, valued at 37,772 British pounds, not much for a person of his achievement and income. The reason for his relatively meager estate was that he had already given most of his literary earnings through his "Agape Fund." Lewis's treatment of neighbors and friends as holy objects epitomized his post-conversion life, a standard drawn from his understanding of Christian hope.

In the Middle Ages, Anselm of Canterbury set up a standard principle of theology—faith seeking understanding—which he used as the basis for his theological methodology: *credo, ut intelligam* ("I believe in order to understand"). This principle holds also for eschatology: *spero, ut intelligam* ("I hope in order to understand"). If it is hope that maintains and upholds faith and keeps it moving forward, if it is hope that draws the believer into

---

11. Lewis, "Weight of Glory," 9.

the life of love, then it will also be hope that becomes the mobilizing and driving force of faith's thinking and reflection on human nature, history, society, and the future of our planet, based on God's promise that for things to be made new, transformation is required. The Christian hope is directed toward the renewal of all things by the God of the resurrection of Jesus Christ. It thereby opens a future outlook that embraces all things, including also the death of former attitudes and agendas, secular and religious alike, because it knows of a "better hope" (Heb. 7:19), a hope bearing not only on the good we desire for ourselves, but also a good desired for others, including our enemies and all living creatures on planet earth. Creative action springing from faith is impossible without new thinking and planning that spring from hope. Hopeful Christians need not be impaired by the perils and enticements of modernity, clinging rigidly to the past or allying themselves with the utopia of the status quo. Rather, believing hope (hope working with faith) will produce resources for the creative, inventive imagination of love.

Summary

When we contemplate the concept of hope, we are pondering the doctrine of eschatology, understood in this study as a "doctrine of hope." Christianity is hopeful about the future, not as wish fulfillment, but as anticipated and fulfilled in Jesus Christ. The future is ours because it belongs to Christ. Hope does not serve the desires of the status quo, but rather the possibilities of newness. In the Bible, the emphasis is always on one's relationship with God. All hope is grounded in God, sustained by God, and directed by God. In the New Testament, hope is not concerned with the realization of human dreams of the future, but with the confidence that waits patiently for God's gifts. As faith has several meanings, so also hope, all relational in nature.

For Discussion and Reflection

1. In your own words, explain the interconnectedness of faith and hope.
2. In your own words, explain the role of hope in spiritual transformation.
3. If hope is said to be related to human volition, what is the first step in the renewal of one's will?

4. If you were to live more hopefully, what personal fear(s) must you dispel?

5. If Christian eschatology is hopeful about the future, what vision fuels your hope for the future of our planet and for humanity as a whole? Thinking beyond the immediate future, what do you envision happening at the end of time? Does God play a role in your scenario?

6. In your understanding, what role does the resurrection of Christ play in Christian eschatology?

7. In your understanding, what role does the concept of "promise" play in the Bible? In your life?

8. Explain and evaluate C. S. Lewis's concept of human "longing" as evidential of the existence of an afterlife.

Chapter 8

The Theological Virtues: Love

Central Idea: The foundational principle of Christian spirituality is that our spiritual health is in proportion to our love for God. Ironically, humans approach God most nearly when they are least like God.

Key Biblical Passages: Leviticus 19:8; Deuteronomy 4:37; 6:5; 7:8; 10:18–19; Psalm 6:4; 33:18, 22, 26; 85:7; 119:41; 130:7; Jeremiah 31:3; Hosea 6:6; Matthew 5:43–46; Mark 12:29–31; Luke 6:27–36; John 3:16; 13:34–35; Romans 5:5, 8; 8:18–39; 13:8; 1 Corinthians 13; 14:1; Galatians 4:19; 5:14; 1 John 4:8, 10

IN THE BEGINNING—LOVE! LOVE is the act of will that at the beginning of time brought forth life. Love—God, energy, Being—is the primal force in the universe. Without love, nothing can exist. With love, all is possible.

Love, like faith and hope, is "the orientation of the individual life toward a center outside of itself, recognizing that my own value is not absolute, but derives from relationship to God. Love, likewise, values other people and things as they are related to God and not as they are useful or important to oneself. Love as a virtue, as a habit of choice and action, consistently does those things that enable others to flourish with their own dignity and their own relationship to God."[1] And that includes organizations, governments, and natural habitats under our care.

Having grown up during the 1960s, I remember Dionne Warwick singing the lyrics penned by Hal David, with music composed by Burt

---

1. Lovin, *Christian Ethics*, 77.

Bacharach: "What the world needs now is love, sweet love. It's the only thing that there's just too little of." Many singers recorded the song, its lyrics haunting and beautiful. I agree with the song's essential proposition, that we need to share more lavishly and compassionately this great resource called love, but is there too little love to go around, or only a misperception to that effect?

Actually, there is plenty of love on this planet, enough for all of us. The reason love seems to be lacking is because love is viewed as a distinct entity, somehow standing alone. If we had a supernatural understanding of love, we would understand that human love is insufficient on its own. It is only adequate for the needs of humanity when it is viewed as part of a triad, intrinsically bound to faith and hope. Like soul cannot survive without body and mind, love cannot thrive without faith and hope. So if we are rooted in faith and hope, we will have love as well.

According to the Bible, love is not something humans produce, or even earn. Love is everywhere, around us and within us, built into the cosmos by a loving Presence. As batteries in our phones and electronic devices need to be renewed regularly, so humans must immerse themselves in this original blessing, renewing their spirit by plugging regularly into God's boundless love, a resource present in every plant, flower, song, person, and situation. All we need to do is connect, absorb, enjoy, and share.

Love is the habit of choosing to be vulnerable by loving the good (what is right), and by acting accordingly. Love is like friendship; when we love our friends, we open ourselves to enjoy them for their own sake, and we wish good things for them. This is the attitude we should have toward creation, its creatures, and toward God. When we allow ourselves to be aware of and open to the goodness in the world, we are drawn to it and want to cherish it, and in this knowing and loving we are happy.

Love is not essentially about being nice or kind or generous; it is not primarily even about others, though such behavior follows. Love is primarily about our relationship with God. Speaking of love, Augustine called it "a movement of the soul toward enjoying God for God's own sake." Likewise, Aquinas speaks of love as "friendship first with God and secondly with all who belong to God." Love, of course, naturally extends to authentic love of self, including our body, mind, personality, and emotions.

In a famous observation, Augustine argued that humanity is not merely created in the image of God, but rather in the image of the Trinity. He developed the idea of relationship within the members of the Trinity, claiming that the three persons are defined by their association to one another. Perhaps the most distinctive element of Augustine's approach was his use of the analogy of love, viewing the Father as the Lover, the Son as the Beloved, and the Spirit as the "bond of love" between the Father and the Son. In like manner, he saw the Spirit as the divine gift which binds believers to God. As the Holy Spirit is the love between the Father and the Son, love is the relationship between rational creatures and the world in which they find themselves. If we humans are the self-awareness of the cosmos, when we love nature and the mysterious cause of its existence we call God, we become like the Holy Spirit, and in this way, happy and fulfilled. We find here an amazing correlation: loving people are happy people; happy people are loving people. This is how we were meant to be.

A Biblical Understanding of Love

The concept of love in the Hebrew Bible (Old Testament) is used with reference to persons as well as actions and things, and there is a profane as well as a religious use. God's love is not depicted emotionally or intellectually but rather as a pointer to God's redeeming activity in human history; hence the focus of Israel's self-awareness on the notion of election, of being chosen. Love is a basic motif in God's dealings with Israel (Exod. 15:13; Deut. 4:37), an electing love always to a degree inexplicable. The bottom line seems to be: "God loves you" (Deut. 7:8). In like manner, God also loves the victims of society, such as the orphan, the widow, and the sojourner (Deut. 10:18–19).

The concept of God's steadfast love is depicted clearly in the prophetic literature, particularly by Hosea but also by Isaiah and Jeremiah. In Jeremiah 31:3, God is said to love Israel with an eternal love, and this love is the basis of God's faithfulness. Hosea reminds us that God desires relationship rather than ritual, intimacy rather than mundane worship: "For I desire steadfast love and not sacrifice, the knowledge of God rather than burnt offerings" (Hos. 6:6).

In the Psalms, Israel hopes in God's love because God is known to be a loving God (Ps. 147:11), watching over those who hope in his love (Ps. 33:18, 22). The expectation of ultimate salvation is the hope in God's covenantal love. God will save because of God's love (Ps. 6:4; 33:26). Indeed, God's salvation and God's love can be spoken of as synonymous (Ps. 85:7; 119:41; 130:7).

The Old Testament idea of the love of God is decisive for the New Testament idea of love. In Mark a Jewish scribe approaches Jesus and asks, "Which commandment is the first of all?" And Jesus answers by quoting from Deuteronomy 6:5 and Leviticus 19:8: "You shall love the Lord your God with all your heart, and with all your soul, and with all your mind, and with all your strength . . . and your neighbor as yourself" (Mark 12:29–31).

As this passage makes clear, God expects total response and commitment from those who claim to love God, even to the point of loving one's enemies (Matt. 5:43–46). This love, which Jesus demands, is to characterize the new people of God, to whom the future belongs. They should show love without expecting it to be returned, lend where there is little hope of repayment, and give without reserve or limit. Indeed, they should do good to those who hate them (Luke 6:27–36). The basis for such radical love is found in God's love, who sent his own Son to demonstrate his love for the world (John 3:16). Surprisingly, in John's Gospel the term "world" is not simply a casual reference to planet earth or to its inhabitants, but rather a technical term that refers to the realm of darkness, which includes all those opposed to God and to God's realm of light; it is that "world" that God loves.

In the New Testament, love is the law of the new order. In fact, those who love others are said to fulfill the law of God (Rom. 13:8; Gal. 5:14). This love is the work of faith, demanded by it, made possible by it, and counted for righteousness on account of it. Yet Paul is emphatic that love does not originate in the human heart, for it is a divine gift, given to the believer by the Holy Spirit. This gift is to be exercised now, in response to God's gracious act in the death and resurrection of Christ and as a sign of the future consummation of that new creation which God has begun in Christ, a fulfillment that is expected in hope (Rom. 5:5).

Love is the primary term describing the result of faith both for the believer and the community in Christ. Because Christ has died and the Holy Spirit has given the community the gift of love, Paul writes that the "love of Christ urges us on" (2 Cor. 5:14), controlling us. In the New Testament, human love is said to originate in God's love, for "God is love" (1 John 4:8). This concept, Christianity's outstanding contribution to world theology and exemplified in Christ, is the reason Jesus gives his followers new marching orders, based on his example: "I give you a new commandment, that you love one another. Just as I have loved you, you also should love one another. By this everyone will know that you are my disciples, if you have love for one another" (John 13:34–35).

In Romans 8:18–39 Paul indicates that love provides personal assurance that in everything God works for good for those who love God, meaning that nothing in creation will be able to separate us from the love of God. For Paul and for Christians in general, the eternal love of God becomes in the love of Christ both the decisive reality in our existence and a world-changing event. Indeed, the work of love is God's goal from the beginning of time.

The Four Loves

Thus far we have used the word "love" freely, without defining it. We have come to the place where we must clarify what we mean by love, for the word is easily misunderstood in the English language. In his classic book, *The Four Loves*, C. S. Lewis examines four words found in the Greek language to describe four basic kinds of love:

1. *Love as Affection (storgē)*: this love refers to familial bonds of love;
2. *Love as Friendship (philia)*: here love refers to companionship, to love between friends;
3. *Love as Romance (eros)*: this love refers primarily to the erotic or sexual bonds of love;
4. *Love as Commitment (agapē)*: here we are speaking of love that is supernatural, spiritual, and unconditional; charitable love.

It is the last of these to which Paul refers in 1 Corinthians 13, using a term traditionally translated as "charity." That translation is misunderstood in today's culture, for it has come to be associated mostly with administering relief to people in need, and that is not what Paul had in mind. Agape is more than generosity and clearly transcends human affection.

Of the four terms for love, the first three generally refer to "love of the deserving," and this is not the meaning Paul wishes to convey. What makes agape unique is that it alone clearly means "love of the undeserving." Biblical scholar N. T. Wright underscores the uniqueness of agape when he argues that, while having something in common with the other loves, agape love goes as far beyond them as sunlight goes beyond candles or even electric light.[2] The classic expression of agape love is Romans 5:8: "But God shows his love for us in that while we were yet sinners Christ died for us." Such love, clearly "love of the undeserving," is rooted in grace.

Can such love be described? Paul attempts to do so in 1 Corinthians 13, saying that "love is patient; love is kind; love is not envious or boastful or arrogant or rude. Love does not insist on its own way; it is not irritable or resentful; it does not rejoice in wrongdoing, but rejoices in the truth. Love bears all things, believes all things, hopes all things, endures all things." If I do not have love, says Paul, "I am nothing"; whatever my privilege, service, or even virtue, if I do not have love, "I gain nothing."

Loving with Agape Love

If agape is a divine quality, can humans participate in such love? To that question the Scriptures answer with a resounding "Yes!" But we must begin, not with mysticism—with the creature's love for God—but at the start of all things, with Love as the divine energy. Herein is agape, "not that we loved God but that he loved us" (1 John 4:10). In God there is no hunger that needs to be filled, only plenteousness that desires to give: "God so loved the world that he gave his only Son" (John 3:16). This is a depiction of God as Lover, the inventor of all loves. C. S. Lewis calls this primal love "Gift-love."

According to Lewis, God, as creator, implants in humans both "Gift-loves" and "Need-loves."[3] Gift-loves are exhibited naturally, such as in the love of a devoted mother or of a benevolent ruler. In addition to these natural gifts, God bestows "Divine Gift-love," working directly in us. Such love enables us to love lavishly or selflessly, including those who are not naturally loveable (lepers, criminals, enemies). God's Gift-love also enables humans to have Need-love toward God. Thus, God's Gift-love bestows on humans a double Need-love:

- supernatural Need-love of God and
- supernatural Need-love of one another.

Remarkably, God turns our need of God into Need-love of God, and stranger still, creates in us an unnatural receptivity of love from our fellow humans. This includes their love for the unlovable in us. Thus God,

---

2. Wright, *1 Corinthians*, 172.
3. Lewis, *Four Loves*, 176.

admitted to the human heart, transforms not only Gift-love but Need-love; not only our Need-love of God, but our Need-love of one another. And that is the task of true spirituality, the invitation to turn our natural loves into agape love, or more specifically, to let God turn our love into agape. Such a task requires renewal of our hearts and minds, a radical change called conversion, which transforms us from "getting" people to "giving" people. This transformation is beyond human possibility. The Christian message is that humans can only experience this makeover when Christ is "formed" in them (Gal. 4:19).

For Lewis, human agape love is not an emotional state but a volitional one, not a state of the feelings but of the will, what we might call "possibility thinking." Agape love is not about liking someone or even about fondness, but rather about "acting as if." In the Bible, one loves God by loving others. And the starting point is to "behave as if" we loved others, because to do so leads to agape. As soon as we engage in such possibility thinking we discover one of life's great truths, that when we behave as if we love someone, we come to love them. The reverse is also true: if we ill-treat others, we come to hate and despise them. And the more cruel we are, the more we will hate—others and God. The key point to remember is that though our feelings for God and others come and go, God's love for us does not.

The foundational principle of Christian spirituality is that our spiritual health is in proportion to our love for God. Ironically, humans approach God most nearly when they are in one sense least like God. For what can be more unlike than fullness and need, sovereignty and humility, righteousness and penitence, limitless power and helplessness? In our love of God, we begin practically, with deeds of kindness, with forgiveness, remembering that good, like evil, increases exponentially. That is why the small decisions we make are of such importance. Writing during World War II, Lewis states: "The smallest good act today is the capture of a strategic point from which, a few months later, you may be able to go on to victories you never dreamed of. An apparently trivial indulgence in lust or anger today is the loss of a ridge or railway line or bridgehead from which the enemy may launch an attack otherwise impossible."[4]

As Lewis reminds us, God, who needs nothing, loves into existence superfluous creatures in order to perfect them. It is easy to acknowledge, but almost impossible to realize for long, that we are mirrors whose brightness, if we are bright, is wholly derived from the sun that shines upon us.

---

4. Lewis, *Mere Christianity*, 117.

God is love, and we can all slowly develop in agape love as we begin to grow in Christ, illumined by natural and supernatural grace.

The Superiority of Agape Love

According to Paul, agape is superior to all virtues, including the supernatural ones: "now faith, hope, and love abide, these three; and the greatest of these is love." Without agape, all spiritual gifts are empty and vain. Earnestly desire the spiritual gifts, we are told in 1 Corinthians 14:1, but make agape your aim.

Agape is superior, says Paul, because love "never ends," meaning literally "love never collapses" (1 Cor. 13:8). Love never fails because it is an extension of God's eternal nature (1 John 4:8). Furthermore, love is superior because while faith and hope are designated for the present life, agape is the way of life in the new creation we await. So to love with agape love now is to live proleptically, out of the resources of the future, and when people live that way, they demonstrate not only the reality of eternal life but the fact that it is available in the present and not merely as a future hope.

Agape, as an attitude of the heart, mind, and will, energizes and activates the whole of one's personality. Agape love is the highest form of knowing, the highest form of being, and the highest form of living. Such love is only possible for those who live in the power of the indwelling Spirit.

We know the story of Mother Teresa, how she devoted her life to serving untouchables in Calcutta. A reporter once asked her the secret of her remarkable ministry, wondering how she accomplished such acts of love. Mother Teresa responded by pointing upward and then saying: "He has done it all. I have done nothing." On another occasion she pointed out that human holiness (namely, our role in God's work of love) does not consist in doing *extraordinary* deeds but rather in doing *ordinary* deeds passionately, with great love.

Faith, hope, and love, these three principles, taken together, are guaranteed to transform our lives. We start with faith, with unconditional trust in God and in God's faithfulness. Faith leads to hope, joyful confidence in the future because God is in charge, and out of that hope comes agape, unconditional "love of the undeserving," manifested fully in Jesus Christ and in all who follow in his steps, including saints like Mother Teresa and like you and me, unworthy yet saved (transformed) by grace.

The Theological Virtues: Love

Summary

Love, like faith and hope, is the orientation of one's life toward a center outside of oneself, recognizing that one's value derives from relationship to God. Love, likewise, values other people and things as they are related to God and not as useful or important to oneself. Love, as a virtue, consistently does those things that enable others to flourish with their own dignity and their own relationship to God. According to Christianity, love is not something humans produce or earn. Love is a gift of grace, built into the cosmos by a loving Presence. Loving may be displayed in acts of kindness, but it is not primarily about others. Love is primarily about one's relationship with God. Those who love the cosmos, including all its creatures and manifestations, are said to be like God, happy and fulfilled. In the New Testament, love is the law of the new order. God's people are to show love unconditionally, without expecting it to be returned. The basis for such love is God's love, evidence in Jesus, God's gift of love for the world. Like faith and hope, love has four meanings, but it is agape, meaning "love of the undeserving," that we envision when we speak of this theological virtue.

For Discussion and Reflection

1. If human love is said to come from divine love, how are these two forms of love similar and how are they different?

2. St. Augustine defined love as "a movement of the soul toward enjoying God for God's own sake." Practically speaking, how does one go about "enjoying God for God's own sake"?

3. St. Augustine famously described the members of the Trinity metaphorically, using the analogy of love. To the best of your ability, explain Augustine's approach, assessing its usefulness as a way to understand the mystery of the Holy Trinity. If necessary, go online or to a library for additional information. Can you think of other analogies that effectively convey the Christian experience of the Trinity?

4. How would you characterize God's love for Israel in the Old Testament?

5. How would you characterize God's love for humanity in the New Testament?

6. If love is said to be related to the human attribute of emotion, what is the first step in the renewal of one's heart?

7. In your own words, explain the meaning of agape love. Why is agape said to be greater than faith and hope?

8. Explain and evaluate C. S. Lewis's concepts of Gift-love and Need-love.

Chapter 10

Growing Graciously

Central Idea: Grace, perhaps life's most transformative concept, is the foundation upon which all morality is based.

Key Biblical Passages: John 3:16; Romans 5:1–5; 6:1; 2 Corinthians 12:9; Philippians 4:13; 1 John 4:19

IN *THE COVENANT*, A novel on South Africa, James Michener introduces a stimulating concept: "Often in the biographies of important women and men," he writes, "one comes across the phrase, 'Like a burst of light, the idea which would animate her life came upon her.'" When the Scriptures exhort us to love the Lord with all our heart, soul, mind, and strength, and our neighbor as ourselves, we come across such a concept, namely, that we are not being asked to try harder or to dig deeper into our own resources. Rather, God's commands are always accompanied by divine resources. The supernatural virtues, available to help us live graciously, are powered by two transformative principles: (a) God never asks of us something we cannot do, and (b) when God is in agreement with us on something, nothing can stop us in our purpose. Paul knew the meaning of those principles, practicing them regularly. As he indicated in Philippians, a hopeful letter written from prison: "I can do all things through [Christ] who strengthens me" (Phil. 4:13). Despite his circumstances, incarcerated falsely and illegally, Paul experienced the grace of God to be active and effective. Harnessed, he writes elsewhere, this power can accomplish most anything: "My grace is sufficient for you, for power is made perfect in weakness" (2 Cor. 12:9).

The Primacy of Grace

Before there was hope, there was faith; before faith, love; before love ... grace! Faith, hope, and love, as habits of choice and action, cannot simply be learned through practice, as other human virtues are. We either have them as gifts of God's grace, or our efforts at the moral life will be limited to the instrumental goodness that a disciplined cultivation of the cardinal virtues makes possible. We have arrived at the primacy of grace, the foundation upon which all morality is based and perhaps life's most transformative concept. The starting point for all virtue is this: we live in a gracious universe, created by Love and perpetuated by Spirit. And this grace is available—already embraces—all creatures, indeed, all life.

Aligned with the tradition that affirms God as creator of the world, we affirm that in God's provision for the beings that issue from God's creativity, grace is built into the processes of birth, of maternal or parental care, and into the orders that humans have developed for the sustenance and maintenance of life. To this grace, which we might call "ordinary grace," we add "extraordinary grace," the unpredictable and unexpected manifestations of divine faith, hope, and love, which bring transformative power to our lives and are part of God's work of righteousness and liberation in our world.

The supernatural virtues are like other virtues in that we see our need of them when we observe the lives of others in whom these virtues are present and especially as we see them embodied in the life of Jesus of Nazareth. But "they cannot be acquired by setting out to learn them. There is an enormous difference between saying to someone, 'See that virtuous person over there. I want you to watch what they do until you can do it also,' and saying, 'You are loved. Now what are you going to do?' Faith, hope, and love must be cultivated in this second way. They can only be acquired in the confidence that they have already been given."[1] As we read in the First Epistle of John: "We love, because he first loved us" (1 John 4:19). That's grace!

Too often people think about faith and hope in a way that locates faith at the beginning and hope at the end of the system. They suppose that those who have faith in God receive a clear set of commandments at the outset, making the moral life a simple matter of doing what we have been told. Or it is supposed that faith in God means belief in a judge who will tally our moral accomplishments at the end and then give us the reward or punishment that we deserve. Ideas like these make it hard for unbelievers

---

1. Lovin, *Christian Ethics*, 77.

to take the Christian moral life seriously or to see that the Christian life also includes freedom, choice, and love. Perhaps worse, such ideas make it difficult for us to understand why our lives include moments of confusion and failure.

Christian faith, however, offers a relationship between God and the moral life quite different from the one often imagined. God meets us not only as lawgiver and judge but primarily as the One who graciously accepts us despite our failure to live up to what the moral life requires, and who restores our hope for the future despite our inability to make up for what society failed to do in the past. We encounter this gracious God both at the beginning of our thinking about ethics and even more precisely in the pain and confusion of actual moral life. If we accept the grace God offers, we are freed from the weight of our past and our hope is restored. If we refuse grace, our moral life is apt to become a deceptive exercise in justifying our mistakes and blaming our failures on others. Or we may slide into the despair of moral failure, unable to undo the wrong we have done and hopeless about our future. Only a gracious God keeps our moral life from becoming a constant measurement of ourselves against a standard we can never meet, anticipating a dreadful judgment we can never escape.

This does not mean that there is no law or judgment in Christian ethics. People have misunderstood God's grace in that way ever since some told Paul that their response to the gospel would be to continue in sin so that grace may abound (Rom. 6:1). It does mean, however, that the moral life is not one long preparation for judgment that lies ahead. The Christian truth is that judgment has already happened, in the death and resurrection of Jesus Christ. And because judgment is covered by grace, we are free to reorient our moral lives toward the future rather than continually reviewing the failures of the past.

When we encounter a gracious God in the midst of life, we can live faithfully, hopefully, and lovingly, perhaps for the very first time. We need no longer live according to someone else's pattern, but we can find the goals and virtues that allow us to live a good life in our own situation, with the abilities and limitations that we actually have. We are free to build relationships and share commitments with others, living by the virtues that make a good life possibly, as we understand them, and not by someone else's rules. So the moral life, instead of being a way to defend ourselves, becomes a way to love our neighbors and God as well.

Correlation between the Eight Virtues
(the Seven Virtues plus Grace)

Romans 5:1–5 is a crucial biblical passage for in it Paul indicates that the supernatural virtues are interrelated not only with one another but also with God's grace, from which they originate. In Romans 5:2 Paul speaks of "this grace in which we stand," as though the whole status of Christians, in their utter dependence on God in Christ, may be described as "grace."

If, as Aquinas surmised, the natural and supernatural virtues complement one another, is it possible to find correlations between them? The following diagram illustrates how this can be done, adding grace to the perimeter of the supernatural virtues, for without grace nothing loving, hopeful, or faithful is possible. Grace symbolizes the character of God; it is from grace that the bountiful universe emerges. With grace we correlate prudence, which represents wisdom and openness to new possibilities. Likewise, love correlates with justice, a virtue of the will. Hope may be said to correlate with fortitude, for both require spiritual bravery. The final correlation is that of faith with temperance, both associated with loyalty, wellbeing, and a balanced lifestyle.

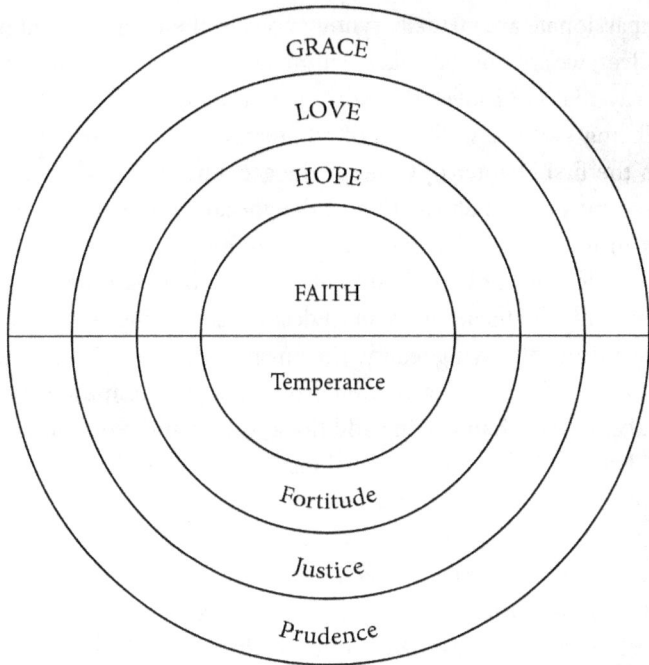

Growing Graciously

There is in every human an impetus which, when nourished, seeks health and wholeness. Physically, emotionally, and cognitively, we are designed for growth. Spiritually, we are designed for transformation. Our happiness is dependent upon growth, upon actualizing our potential. That truth was affirmed by ancient philosophers such as Plato and Aristotle and refined spiritually by medieval Christian theologians such as Augustine and Aquinas.

Grace has endowed us with the physical and spiritual potential for growth, but also with an innate longing for God. As Augustine stated in the famous passage from the *Confessions*: "You have made us for Yourself, and our hearts are restless until they find rest in You."

By now it should be clear that the character of God, indeed that the nature of reality, is gracious, loving, and compassionate. God (whether called Father, the Infinite, the Tao, Brahman, or Being) is life-giving and life-affirming, willing our transformation and the transformation of the world and involved in those transformations. The words gracious, loving, and compassionate are virtually synonymous in the Bible. We did not create ourselves; we are not self-made. Ultimately, all we are and have are gifts.

To say that God loves the world (John 3:16) means that God wills our wellbeing and the wellbeing of all creation. In the story of creation, found in the first chapter of Genesis, the account of each day of creation is followed by a divine affirmation of the goodness of what has been created. Because of the tendency of humans to fall short of their God-given potential, a deeper life with God is offered. On our part, such a relation must be intentional, meaning we must desire a deepening relationship with this powerful and all-loving reality. The image of the Christian life that goes with this view of God is quite different from the legalistic approach so many people take. Rather than placing additional duties and requirements upon us, the Christian life is about a relationship with God that transforms us into more compassionate beings. This is another way to speak of the grace of God.

Healthy human being are said to go through discernable stages of growth throughout their lifetime. As humans grow by progressing physically, psychologically, emotionally, and even intellectually, so they undergo stages of growth in their faith. What Erik Erikson contributed to our understanding of the stages of psychosocial development, Jean Piaget to the stages of cognitive development, and Lawrence Kohlberg to the stages of moral development, so James Fowler did for spirituality in developing seven stages of faith, from stage zero, called "primal faith," when infants and toddlers develop (or fail to develop) a sense of safety about the universe and the divine, to a sixth stage called "universalizing faith," a rarely reached stage of those who live their lives to the full in service of others without any real fears or worries. Most people plateau at what Fowler calls the "synthetic-conventional" stage, one arising in adolescence. At this stage authority is usually placed in individuals or groups that represent one's beliefs.[2]

Fowler's stages of faith are listed below, followed by M. Scott Peck's simplified version:

Stage 0: *Primal Faith* (0 to 2 years): This stage is characterized by early learning the safety of the environment. Under consistent nurture, children develop a sense of safety about the universe and the divine. Negative experiences (neglect and abuse) lead to distrust of the universe and the divine.

---

2. Fowler, *Stages of Faith*.

Stage 1: *Intuitive-Projective* (3 to 7 years): This is the stage of preschool children in which fantasy and reality often are mixed together. However, during this stage, our most basic ideas about God are usually learned from our parents and/or society.

Stage 2: *Mythic-Literal* (mostly in school children): When children become school-age, they start understanding the world in more logical ways. They generally accept the stories told to them by their faith community but tend to understand them in very literal ways. [Some people remain in this stage through adulthood.]

Stage 3: *Synthetic-Conventional* (arising in adolescence; ages 12 to adulthood): Most people move on to this stage as teenagers. At this point, their lives have grown to include several different social circles, which they need to pull together. When this happens, a person usually adopts some sort of all-encompassing belief system. However, at this stage, people tend to have a hard time seeing outside their box, not recognizing that they are "inside" a belief system. At this stage, authority is usually placed in individuals or groups that represent one's beliefs. [A great many adults remain in this stage.]

Stage 4: *Individuative-Reflective* (usually mid-twenties to late thirties): This is the tough stage, often begun in young adulthood, when people start seeing outside the box and realizing that there are other "boxes." They begin to examine their beliefs critically on their own and often become disillusioned with their former faith. Ironically, the Stage 3 people usually think that Stage 4 people have become "backsliders" when in reality they have actually moved forward.

Stage 5: *Conjunctive Faith* (mid-life crisis): It is rare for people to reach this stage before mid-life. This is the point when people begin to realize the limits of logic and start to accept life's paradoxes. As they begin to see life as a mystery, they often return to sacred stories and symbols but this time without remaining in a theological box.

Stage 6: *Universalizing Faith* (enlightened stage): Few people reach this stage; those who do, live their lives to the full in service of others without real worry or spiritual doubt.

Living Graciously on Planet Earth

M. Scott Peck's Simplified Version[3]

I. *Chaotic-Antisocial*—People in this stage are usually self-centered and often find themselves in trouble due to unprincipled living. If they do finally embrace the next stage, it often occurs in a very dramatic way.

II. *Formal-Institutional*—At this stage people rely on some sort of institution (such as a church) to give them stability. They become attached to the forms of their religion and become extremely upset when these are called into question.

III. *Skeptic-Individual*—Those who break with the previous stage usually do so when they start seriously questioning previously held values and beliefs. Frequently they end up non-religious and some stay here permanently.

IV. *Mystical-Communal*—People who reach this stage start to realize that there is truth to be found in the previous two stages and that life can be paradoxical and mysterious. Emphasis is placed more on community rather than on individual concerns.

Faith, we have discovered, is a way of knowing and a way of growing. What holds true for faith also holds true for hope and love. And as we grow in faith, hope, and love, we grow in grace. The task of today's church, mosque, and synagogue—of all religious institutions—is to nurture the natural and supernatural virtues, not in isolation, but in harmony, instilling in their members trust in the sacred, compassion for one another, and a hopeful vision for the community of nations and for the future of our planet.

As we grow in this endeavor, citizens on this planet will become better stewards of its resources, resulting in less selfishness, greed, violence, fear, and complacency; with parents like that, young people will become less abusive, addictive, disappointed, restless, and bored. As we grow in grace, we will discover purpose in life, living as God intends: healthier and happier. And planet earth will be grateful.

The Enneagram: A Model for Growth[4]

Recently I began using a model for self-understanding and growth called the Enneagram (pronounced ANY-a-gram). The word Enneagram stems

---

3. Peck, *A Different Drum*.
4. For knowledge of the Enneagram I am indebted to the contributions of Don R.

from the Greek *ennea*, meaning "nine" and *grammos*, meaning "points." The Enneagram refers to a nine-pointed star diagram that can be used to map out nine fundamental personality types of human nature and their complex interrelationships.

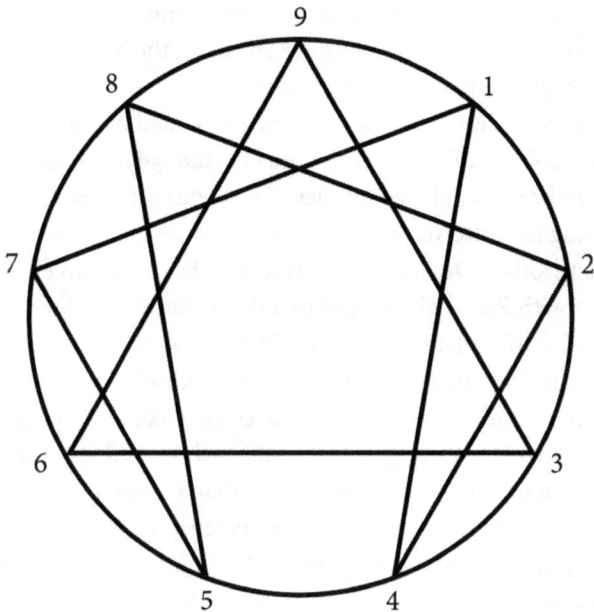

The diagram consists of three interrelated symbols: a circle, a triangle, and a hexad.

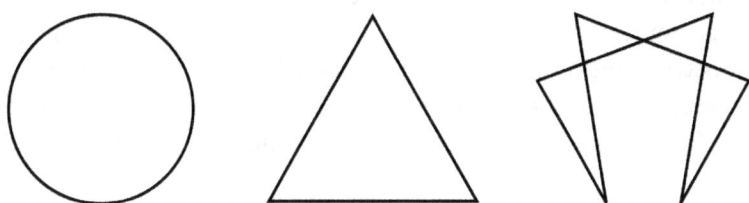

Riso and Russ Hudson; David N. Daniels and Virginia A. Price; and Richard Rohr and Andreas Ebert. For more information, consult the bibliography or visit their websites online.

The Enneagram is a means to initiate a process of inquiry that can lead individuals to profound truths about themselves and their place in the world. While knowing one's personality type provides important information, that information is merely an embarkation point for a much greater journey, the journey into happiness and wholeness.

The origins of the Enneagram are uncertain, though parallels have been found in the Jewish Tree of Life (Kabbalah), the Muslim Sufi tradition, the Hindu yogic chakra tradition, and in the Christian monastic tradition of the Orthodox Church, particularly as articulated by the fourth-century Orthodox theologian Evagrius of Pontus (c. 348–399), a desert monk who taught his followers yogic techniques of concentration, including identifying psychological patterns that keep human beings locked in inner turmoil. Evagrius and other Desert Elders were familiar with Greek philosophy, particularly with Plato, who taught that the material world was a reflection of a spiritual world. Plato also quoted Pythagoras as saying, "All the world can be explained by the numbers one through nine."

The term Enneagram was introduced by George I. Gurdjieff (1879–1949), an Armenian-born spiritual teacher who traveled widely in search of esoteric practices helpful in opening human consciousness. He brought these practices to his study groups in St. Petersburg and Moscow in 1916, calling his principles of inner growth The Fourth Way. When Gurdjieff brought the symbol of the Enneagram to the West, it was seen to contain the interweaving of two fundamental cosmic laws, the Law of Seven (also called the Law of World Maintenance), which explains that all change in the universe follows seven distinct stages before reaching its completion, and the Law of Three (also called the Law of World Creation), a ternary system which explains that all complete phenomena are composed of three separate sources, two polarities and a third mediating or reconciling principle between them. Since ternary systems seek completion in newness, the interweaving of the three sources produces a fourth force or realm of possibility. These laws were said to apply to everything in the universe, including humanity.

Building on the Law of Three, Gurdjieff argued for only three "personality types," not nine, which he described as "essence types" rather than as "personality types." For Gurdjieff, "essence" is what one is from birth, whereas personality is what one acquires through external conditioning. Furthermore, one's essence type is not intended to be one's permanent identity, but merely the starting point for a pathway of transformation that unfolds according to the Law of Three. Whether one begins the journey as number 1, 2, or 3 of the essence types, the goal is to strengthen and transforms these three lower centers so that one becomes a new being at number 4 (a state Gurdjieff described as a "balanced" person).

In the late 1960s Oscar Ichazo, a Bolivian spiritual therapist teaching in Chile, developed a new use of the Enneagram, correlating its nine points to the seven deadly sins by adding fear and vanity. He joined forces with Claudio Naranjo, a Chilean psychiatrist working in California, and their collaboration resulted in the birth of the modern Enneagram personality movement. Using the Enneagram as a tool for personality typing, the modern movement has largely abandoned Gurdjieff's core understanding of the diagram as a cosmic symbol.

While the Enneagram has proved to be a valuable transformative device, it has also come under considerable criticism, mostly from conservative religious leaders such as Father Mitch Pacwa, S. J., a former practitioner, who cautions against its use on the grounds of gnostic and occult roots (including contributions by questionable contributors such as G. I. Gurdjieff and Oscar Ichazo), its deterministic approach (categorizing people into nine unverifiable personality types), and its lack of adequate scientific validation.

Human movements, particularly at their inception, frequently come under criticism or misunderstanding, fueled, if not by ignorance, by bias and fear. Of course, any system or technique can be abused, by deceitful and by well-intentioned leaders alike. This can be true of all organizations, whether psychological, social, political, or religious. Of course such abuse, when verified, must be condemned and eliminated. In my estimation, the strength of the modern Enneagram movement is that it can be used by religious and irreligious people alike. While aspects of the Enneagram have been promoted by religious individuals, it is not a religion, as some have declared, but rather a heuristic tool.

To those who fault the Enneagram as poor science or as pop psychology, the answer is that this movement is a work in progress, seeking validation through scientific research and experimentation. The Enneagram is essentially an oral movement—people helping people; it is neither secretive nor deterministic. When used reasonably and without religious or occult pretensions, the Enneagram helps people identify problems and fixations in their lives, including paths for growth. When used properly, the Enneagram is not deterministic. Rather than place people into boxes, it allows them to see the boxes they have created and how they can mature further. The Enneagram allows for hundreds if not thousands of personality permutations within its typology, not nine simplistic boxes for pigeonholing people.

It is evident that among those who criticize the Enneagram's holistic approach are religious purists and supremacists who, fearing loss of control, proclaim a monopoly on happiness and truth. Healthy living in the twenty-first century encourages us to be open to diversity, living courageously rather than fearfully. There are many spiritual dangers in our world today, but we will not move ahead by digging wider moats or by reconstituting medieval weaponry. We need to face the future together. The Enneagram is part of the solution, not part of the problem. Those who question its validity need not prevent others from utilizing its benefits.

One of the most challenging notions for us to accept initially about transformational work is that personality—the ego and its structures—is an artificial construct. Until now, our personality seems to have been our entire reality. Identifying with our personality has been how we have lived and gotten by in life. But as we examine our personality more objectively, we realize that it consists largely of a collection of internal defenses and reactions, deeply ingrained beliefs and habits about the self and the world that have come from the past, particularly from our childhood. In the past our personality has helped us cope and survive, but upon adult reflection, we see its limitation. This personality has served as a mask, creating both a mistaken identity and an illusion of permanence.

In most cases the personality has created survival techniques such as anger, resentment, shame, and envy as protective mechanisms for the ego, but in the process, these attitudes hid or covered our spiritual core. In addition, the painful events of early childhood created certain ways of interpreting our experiences, so that later life events reinforce our beliefs about our self and our world. As a result of this reinforcement of our earliest sense of self, our personality thickened, perpetuating certain patterns around which our identity revolves.

The personality is highly automatic, and it leads us into repetitive patterns and problems. But the personality is only automatic when we are not aware of it. With awareness come power, wisdom, energy, and strength. Learning to let go of the protective patterns of our personality enables us to be more present and awake, more energized and alive.

According to the Enneagram, inner transformational work proceeds layer by layer, from the most external forms of personality to the inner core of our being. The automatic pattern of our personality draws us outward, but by bringing awareness to these patterns, we can reverse the course. Willing to know the truth about what is really occurring in us dissolves the structures in which we are trapped.

The Enneagram encourages us to become aware of our personality type, including our strengths and weaknesses (virtues and vices), and provides discernable stages for growth.

According to medieval Christian thinking, humans are tempted by the seven deadly sins: lust, gluttony, greed, sloth, anger, envy, and pride. To defeat the seven deadly vices Christians were to practice the seven heavenly virtues, identified as chastity, abstinence, liberality, diligence, patience, kindness, and humility.[5] Adding two vices (deceit and fear) to the traditional notion of the Seven Deadly Sins, the Enneagram identifies nine "Passions": Anger, Pride, Deceit, Envy, Avarice (greed), Fear, Gluttony, Lust, and Sloth. These represent the nine main ways that we lose our center and become distorted in our thinking, feeling, and doing.

For those unfamiliar with the Enneagram or who wish additional information, the following unit describes the nine personality types, including their primary virtues and vices (Passions).[6]

Type One: *The Perfectionist* (Reformer). Ones are ethical and conscientious, with a strong sense of right and wrong. Their primary virtue is *Prudence*, Sobriety, or objectivity. They are teachers and crusaders, always striving to improve things but afraid of making a mistake. Well-organized, orderly, and fastidious, they try to maintain high standards but can slip into being critical and perfectionistic. Their primary Passion is *Anger*, not overt anger, but repressed anger, leading to frustration, impatience, and dissatisfaction with themselves and with the world. At their best, healthy Ones are wise, discerning, realistic, and noble, as well as morally heroic. Unhealthy Ones tend to be dogmatic, inflexible, opinionated, judgmental self-righteous condemning and compulsive.

Type Two: *The Helper* (Giver). Twos are empathetic, sincere, and warm-hearted. Their primary virtue is *Humility*. They are friendly, generous, and self-sacrificing, but they can also be sentimental, flattering, and

---

5. The seven heavenly virtues are defined in appendix B.

6. Riso and Hudson, *Wisdom of the Enneagram*, 11–12, 23, 97–340; see also *Personality Types*.

people-pleasing. They are driven to be close to others, and they often do things for others in order to be needed. They typically have problems taking care of themselves and acknowledging their own needs. Their primary Passion is *Pride*, better described as Vainglory—pride in their own virtue. At their best, healthy Twos are unselfish and altruistic and have unconditional love for themselves and others. Unhealthy Twos tend to be self-serving, resentful, manipulative, possessive, coercive, victimized, and entitled.

Type Three: *The Achiever* (Performer). Threes are self-assured, attractive, and charming. Their primary virtue is *Truthfulness*. Ambitious, competent, and energetic, they can also be status-conscious and highly driven for personal advancement. Threes are often concerned about their image and what others think of them. They typically have problems with workaholism and competitiveness. Their primary passion is *Vanity* or deceit, putting effort into developing their ego instead of their true nature. At their best, healthy Threes are self-accepting, authentic, and everything they seem to be—role models who inspire others. Unhealthy Threes tend to be narcissistic, exhibitionist, vindictive, exploitative, deceptive, and career-addicted.

Type Four: *The Individualist* (Romantic). Fours are self-aware, sensitive, reserved, and quiet. Their primary virtue is *Self-Control*. They are self-revealing, emotionally honest, and personal, but they can also be moody and self-conscious. Withholding themselves from others due to feeling vulnerable and defective, they can also feel disdainful and exempt from ordinary ways of living. They typically have problems with self-indulgence and self-pity. Their primary Passion is *Envy*, feeling that others possess qualities that they lack. At their best, healthy Fours are inspired and highly creative, able to renew themselves and transform their experiences. Unhealthy Fours tend to be moody, narcissistic, hypersensitive, self-indulgent, despairing, decadent, alienated, and depressed.

Type Five: *The Investigator*. Fives are alert, insightful, and curious. Their primary virtue is *Detachment*. They are able to concentrate and focus on developing complex ideas and skills. Independent and innovative, they can become preoccupied with their thoughts and imaginary constructs. They become detached, yet high-strung and intense. They typically have problems with isolation, eccentricity, and nihilism. Their primary Passion is *Avarice*. At their best, healthy Fives are visionary pioneers, often ahead of their time and able to see the world in an entirely new way. Unhealthy Fives tend to be reclusive, isolated, scornful, eccentric, nihilistic, dissociative, and delusional.

Type Six: *The Loyalist*. Sixes are reliable, hardworking, and responsible, but they can also be defensive, evasive, and highly anxious—running on stress while complaining about it. Their primary virtue is *Courage*. They are often cautious and indecisive but can also be reactive, defiant, and rebellious. They typically have problems with self-doubt and suspicion. Their primary Passion is *Fear* or anxiety about possible future events. At their best, healthy Sixes are internally stable, self-confident, and self-reliant, courageously supporting the weak and powerless. Unhealthy Sixes tend to be unreliable, evasive, self-doubting, paranoid, aggressive, panicky, and cowardly.

Type Seven: *The Enthusiast*. Sevens are versatile, optimistic, and spontaneous. Their primary virtue is *Temperance* or moderation. Playful, high-spirited, and practical, they can also be overextended, scattered, and undisciplined. They constantly seek new and exciting experiences, but they can become distracted and exhausted by staying on the go. They typically have problems with superficiality and impulsiveness. Their primary Passion is *Gluttony* or intemperance, feeling that they never have enough. At their best, healthy Sevens focus their talents on worthwhile goals, becoming joyous, highly accomplished, and full of gratitude. Unhealthy Sevens tend to be unfocused, impetuous, excessive, reckless, and panic-stricken.

Type Eight: *The Challenger*. Eights are self-confident, strong, and assertive. Their primary virtue is *Justice* or innocence. Protective, resourceful, and decisive, they can also be proud and domineering. Eights feel that they must control their environment, often becoming confrontational and intimidating. They typically have problems with allowing themselves to be close to others. Their primary Passion is *Lust* or need for control. At their best, healthy Eights are self-mastering—they use their strength to improve others' lives, becoming heroic, magnanimous, and sometimes historically great. Unhealthy Eights tend to be proud, egocentric, defiant, vengeful, domineering, violent, destructive, and tyrannical.

Type Nine: *The Peacemaker*. Nines are accepting, trusting, and stable. Their primary virtue is *Fortitude* or emotional stability. They are good-natured, kind-hearted, easygoing, and supportive but can also be too willing to go along with others to keep the peace. They want everything to be without conflict but can tend to be complacent and minimize anything upsetting. They typically have problems with passivity and stubbornness. Their primary

Passion is *Sloth*, not as in laziness, but in their desire to be unaffected by life. At their best, healthy Nines are indomitable and all-embracing; they are able to bring people together and heal conflicts. Unhealthy Nines tend to be disengaged, unreflective, irresponsible, stubborn, resentful, fatalistic, and disoriented.

The purpose of the Enneagram is not to help us get rid of our personality, but rather to utilize our personality to recognize that it is only a small part of the totality of who we are. The Enneagram provides access to the wisdom we need to let go of the limiting mechanisms of our personality so that we can more deeply experience our essential self.

The mechanism of the personality is set in motion by what we call the *Basic Fear* of each type.[7] This fear arises during early childhood. As the result of unmet infant needs and subsequent blockages, we inevitably come to the conclusion that there is something wrong with us; this unconscious anxiety is called our Basic Fear. While we can recognize the Basic Fears of all nine types in ourselves, our own type's Basic Fear motivates our behavior more than the others.

As wisdom has always recognized, the agendas of our egos are ultimately self-defeating: *Ones* strive to maintain personal integrity but still feel divided and at war with themselves; *Twos* spend their lives searching for love from others and still feel that they are unloved; *Threes* pursue achievement and recognition but still feel worthless and empty; *Fours* spend their lives trying to discover the meaning of their personal identity and still do not know who they are; *Fives* accumulate knowledge and skills and build up their confidence but still feel helpless and incapable; *Sixes* toil to create security for themselves and still feel anxious and fearful about the world; *Sevens* look high and low for happiness but still feel unhappy and frustrated; *Eights* do everything in their power to protect themselves and their interests but still feel vulnerable and threatened; *Nines* sacrifice a great deal to achieve inner peace and stability but still feel ungrounded and insecure.

To compensate for the Basic Fear, a *Basic Desire* arises. The Basic Desire is the way that we defend against our Basic Fear in order to continue to function. The Basic Desire is what we believe will make us okay. The Basic Desire may be called the ego agenda, because it tells us what the ego self is striving after. Thus we might say that the whole of personality structure is composed of our flight from our Basic Fear and our single-minded pursuit of our Basic Desire.

---

7. Riso and Hudson, *Wisdom of the Enneagram*, 30–33.

Type 1: the desire to have integrity (deteriorates into critical perfectionism)

Type 2: the desire to be loved (deteriorates into the need to be needed)

Type 3: the desire to be valuable (deteriorates into chasing after success)

Type 4: the desire to be oneself (deteriorates into self-indulgence)

Type 5: the desire to be competent (deteriorates into useless specialization)

Type 6: the desire to be secure (deteriorates into an attachment to beliefs)

Type 7: the desire to be happy (deteriorates into frenetic escapism)

Type 8: the desire to protect oneself (deteriorates into constant fighting)

Type 9: the desire to be at peace (deteriorates into stubborn neglectfulness)[8]

According to the Enneagram, if we are to find happiness, we must let go of the familiar and embrace the unfamiliar. Each person lies along or on one of nine Levels of Development; three levels are described as healthy, three as average, and three as unhealthy. People in the healthy range are able to move in their Direction of Integration (toward self-actualization, letting go of old habitual patterns and moving toward a richer, fuller life), while those in the average to unhealthy range "act out" in the Direction of Disintegration ("their path of least resistance").

Under conditions of increased stress and anxiety, types in their average to unhealthy range of behavior will begin to exhibit or "act out" some of the average or unhealthy behaviors of the type in their Direction of Disintegration. A person tends to act out of the behavior in the type in his or her *Direction of Disintegration* at roughly the same level at which they are functioning in their own type:

Methodical Ones become moody and irrational as average or unhealthy Fours;

Needy Twos become aggressive and dominating as average or unhealthy Eights;

Driven Threes become disengaged and apathetic as average or unhealthy Nines;

Aloof Fours become overinvolved and clinging as average or unhealthy Twos;

---

8. Ibid., 33.

Detached Fives become hyperactive and scattered as average or unhealthy Sevens;

Dutiful Sixes become competitive and arrogant as average or unhealthy Threes;

Scattered Sevens become perfectionistic and critical as average or unhealthy Ones;

Self-confident Eights become secretive and fearful as average or unhealthy Fives;

Complacent Nines become anxious and worried as average or unhealthy Sixes.[9]

The Direction of Disintegration is said to be unconscious and compulsive (the ego's way of automatically compensating for psychic imbalance), while moving in the Direction of Integration requires conscious choice. When we are on the path of integration, we are saying to ourselves: "In want to grow and be happy, and to do so, I must live intentionally." As we become familiar with our inner baggage, the very qualities we need for our growth become accessible to us, speeding the progress of liberation from the patterns of our personality.

In a sense, one can think of each personality type as flowing into another, marking a further development of the prior type, much as the Direction of Disintegration marks a type's further entanglement in conflicted ego states. The *Direction of Integration* is a natural outgrowth of the healthiest qualities of that type.

Ones need to overcome their criticality and rigidity by moving toward the joy and enthusiasm of healthy *Sevens*; *Twos* need to overcome their tendency to deceive themselves about their need, feelings, and motives by moving toward the self-understanding and emotional honesty of healthy *Fours*; *Threes* need to overcome their desire to surpass others and draw attention to themselves by moving toward the commitment and humility of healthy *Sixes*; *Fours* need to overcome their moodiness and self-indulgence by moving toward the integrity and self-discipline of healthy *Ones*; *Fives* need to overcome their detachment and cynicism by moving toward the practicality and courage of healthy *Eights*; *Sixes* need to overcome their pessimism and suspicion of others by moving toward the hopefulness and receptivity of healthy *Nines*; *Sevens* need to overcome their superficiality and impulsiveness by moving toward the depth and focus of healthy *Fives*;

9. Ibid., 89.

Eights need to overcome their emotional armoring and egocentricity by moving toward the compassion and concern for others of healthy *Twos*; *Nines* need to overcome their complacency and self-forgetting by moving toward the energy and self-investment of healthy *Threes*.[10]

Ultimately the goal is to move completely around the Enneagram, integrating what each type symbolizes and acquiring the active use of the healthy potentials of all the types. The ideal is to become a balanced, fully functioning human being, and each of the types symbolizes a different important aspect of what we need to achieve this end. In a sense, self-transcendence is a rebirth, a true transformation, a coming into being of a new person, leaving the old ways behind and striking forth into unknown territory.

While the Enneagram has captured the popular imagination, traditional practitioners are wary of the modern Enneagram movement. While some more spiritually oriented Enneagram teachers are now emphasizing transformative movement over diagnostic typology, as Gurdjieff did, they are said to bypass the Enneagram's cosmic nature, "borrowing the exterior forms of [the] symbol without grasping its interior dynamic."[11] This becomes evident in the diagram itself, which contains a peculiarity: the triangle (the figure tracing the numbers 3–6–9) and the hexad (the figure tracing the numbers 1–4–2–8–5–7) do not interact. According to the Enneagram, if you identify as a One, Two, Four, Five, Seven, or Eight, you will progress or regress (Direction of Integration or Disintegration) following the pattern 1–4–2–8–5–7. If you identify as a Three, Six, or Nine, you only cycle through these three points. Since the two sets fail to interact directly, the use of the Enneagram for personality typing is said to be faulty because such use "inadvertently collapses the diagram and its possibilities into a set of two closed circles," repeating patterns endlessly and mechanically, "like a dog chasing its tail."[12]

While this problem may be disconcerting for those who use the Enneagram as a process model, it is not insuperable, for in addition to a triangle and a hexad, the Enneagram features a circle, used universally to depict unity and wholeness. Utilizing the Enneagram as a spiritual tool, Don Riso and Russ Hudson have developed "the Enneagram of Letting Go," a nine-step pattern for letting go of troublesome habits or defensive patterns that follows

---

10. Ibid., 92.
11. Moore, *Gurdjieff*, 345.
12. Bourgeault, *Holy Trinity and the Law of Three*, 56.

the diagram's holistic circumference rather than the disengaged symbols embedded within.[13] Whether you follow the Direction of Integration, substitute a nine-step pattern, or develop your own use of the Enneagram, the diagram's use as a transformative tool is practically limitless.

The title of Tilda Norberg's introductory book on Gestalt Pastoral Care, *Consenting to Grace*, summarizes my understanding of the Christian way of life, for "consenting to grace" is how we are called to live on planet earth. No better statement on living graciously has been penned than the words attributed to St. Francis of Assisi:

> Lord, make me an instrument of thy peace.
> Where there is hatred, let me sow love;
> Where there is injury, pardon; where there is doubt, faith;
> Where there is despair, hope; where there is darkness, light;
> Where there is sadness, joy.
> O divine Master, grant that I may not so much seek to be consoled as to console,
> To be understood as to understand; To be loved as to love;
> For it is in giving that we receive;
> It is in pardoning that we are pardoned;
> It is in dying to self that we are born to eternal life.

Summary

The starting point for all virtue is this: we live in a gracious universe, created by Love and perpetuated by Spirit. As we read in the First Epistle of John, "We love, because [God] first loved us." This does not mean that there is no law or judgment in Christian ethics, for the Christian truth is that judgment has already happened, in the death and resurrection of Jesus Christ. And because judgment is covered by grace, we are free to reorient our moral lives toward the future rather than on the failures of the past. When we encounter a gracious God in the midst of life, we can live faithfully, hopefully, and lovingly, perhaps for the very first time. Spiritually, we are designed for transformation. The moral life prepares and empowers us for growth. As humans grow physically, psychologically, emotionally, and cognitively, so they undergo various stages of growth in their faith. The

---

13. Riso and Hudson, *Wisdom of the Enneagram*, 363–66.

chapter examines two such models, James Fowler's stages of faith and the Enneagram, a model for self-understanding and spiritual growth.

For Discussion and Reflection

1. When you ponder the moral life, do you begin with the concept of commandments, rewards, and punishments, or with grace? What difference does your starting point make in your actions and motivation?

2. Paul's greatest experience of God's grace occurred in times of hardship and duress. Have you experienced similar manifestations of grace? If so, put your experience in writing and share it with others.

3. Do you agree with the text about the primacy of grace? Where would you place grace in the hierarchy of virtues?

4. When Christians speak of the primacy of grace, whether God's grace to us or our demonstration of grace to others, is this approach helpful in today's aggressive and unforgiving culture? Are displays of compassion and grace, particularly toward enemies, criminals, and indigents, signs of weakness or of strength? How does your answer square with Paul's statement in 2 Corinthians 12:9?

5. Assess the correlation between the virtues as illustrated in the diagram of the eight virtues. What changes might you make to enhance the meaning of these concepts and their interrelationships?

6. James Fowler developed seven stages of faith, from primal faith in infancy to the rarely reached stage he called "universalizing faith." Do you find this approach to faith helpful? Where do you see yourself in this configuration?

7. Do you find M. Scott Peck's version of the stages of faith helpful or overly simplistic? Explain your answer.

8. After reading about the Enneagram, which of the nine personality types best matches your self-understanding? What do you see as your primary virtue? What do you see as your primary vice? On the basis of your reading about the Enneagram, what pathway represents your Direction of Integration?

Epilogue

Realized Eschatology

Central Idea: A common Christian response to current problems is to long for Christ's return to reward faith and destroy evil. While the Bible promises renewal and redemption, we need not wait for these to occur at the end of time. Rather, according to a perspective known as "realized eschatology," the fulfillment of God's promises is possible in the present.

Key Biblical Passages: Matthew 5:13–16; 6:10, 33; 7:7–8; 8:20; 12:28; 13:30–32; 25:34; Mark 1:15; 11:23; Luke 12:31–32; 17:20–21; John 3:17–21, 31–36; 5:28–29; 6:47; 12:48; 18:36; 2 Corinthians 1:20; 5:5; 6:2; Hebrews 4:7; Revelation 21:1, 5

THERE ARE A GREAT many problems on planet earth these days, ecological, social, political, and economic, and a common Christian response is to long for Christ's return to judge the earth and take believers to heaven. Non-believers often associate such hope with wish-fulfillment, calling it "pie in the sky by and by." Is Christianity escapist? Are its solutions to world problems futuristic, impractical, and unrealistic? For the answer, people often turn to the doctrine of eschatology, an aspect of theology that deals with the end-times and the "eschaton," a Greek word meaning "the end of history" or "the final event."

If eschatology is the study of "final things," it would be easy to believe that God's promises of renewal and redemption, whether of nature or of humanity, will occur at the end of time, when the new heaven and the new earth are revealed. Such thinking, however, is not biblical. One aspect of

Realized Eschatology

eschatology that is often ignored or overlooked is known as "realized eschatology," a view associated with the British biblical scholar C. H. Dodd. This outlook speaks of final things as being with us now. A life with God is possible in the present, even though that final life in all its fullness has not yet arrived.

Scholars speak of a tension in the New Testament between "the already and the not yet," meaning that God's long-awaited eschatological transformation of reality, including the coming of the Kingdom of God and the judgment of evil and reward of faith (eternal life), is underway in the present, initiated by Jesus' coming into the world and later in the coming of the Holy Spirit.

Proponents of "realized eschatology" note that according to the Gospels, Jesus began his ministry by announcing that the time had come for God to begin God's reign on earth, and that the first Christians understood this was happening in Jesus' own person and work. The Good News of the gospel was not that the Kingdom was about to be realized on earth, but that the Kingdom had actually arrived, and that its power was already present: "For, in fact, the kingdom of God is among [or within] you" (Luke 17:21).

According to Mark's Gospel, the preaching ministry of Jesus was eschatological in nature, summarized by the New Revised Standard Version as: "The time is fulfilled, and the kingdom of God *has come near*" (Mark 1:15). Earlier versions, including the King James and the Revised Standard Version, translate the Greek word rendered "has come near" differently: "the kingdom of God *is at hand*." To say that the Kingdom "has come near," as later versions correctly indicate, means that God's reign is uniquely available in Christ. This does not mean, however, that it is fully here, as C. H. Dodd maintained, arguing for the translation "the kingdom of God *has come*," or that the Kingdom was only available in the first century, or in Palestine, Israel, or in any other specific territory on earth.

The phrase "Kingdom of God," a concept found in the Lord's Prayer ("Thy Kingdom come, Thy will be done, on earth as it is in heaven") and throughout the Gospels, is often misunderstood as referring to an earthly institution such as the Church, or to a geographical territory or state such as the Vatican, but as the prayer tells us, using a traditional Hebrew literary style known as "synonymous parallelism," the Kingdom of God is present on earth wherever and whenever God's will is as fully done as it is in heaven. That is to say, to do the will of God and to be in the Kingdom are one and the same thing. Hence it might be better to speak of the "rule" or "reign" of God rather than the "kingdom" of God. While Jesus' Jewish audience understood God's coming rule in terms of material prosperity, political power, and national greatness, that is not what Jesus intended. When Jesus is quoted as saying to Pilate, "My kingdom is not from (of) this world" (John 18:36), Jesus meant that his rule was unlike other worldly kingdoms, political, material, or national in nature. On the positive side, equating the "Kingdom of God" with the "will of God" indicates the universality of God's rule. There are no racial, social, or gender distinctions in God's rule, no favored peoples or nations.

Furthermore, this emphasis has powerful ethical implications. The notion of God's rule on earth challenges all attachments to centers of value and power that serve egocentric impulses. Divine primacy relativizes all idolatries—including the gods of nation, self, class, family, race, gender, institution, success, money, sexuality, and even religion—to the status of proximal goods. Any claim of ultimacy for them or by them must be avoided or relinquished. This means that social distinctions by which humans define themselves have only relative value and therefore are not indicative of ultimate value or worth.[1]

To pray "Thy Kingdom come" is not to imply, however, that God's rule is not here, for God's Kingdom is always present in seed form, always near and growing. That is why for Jesus the growth of the mustard seed, the smallest of seeds, into a tree symbolized the Kingdom (Matt. 13:31–32). Our actions can delay the Kingdom and hinder its power, but the Kingdom will be near until its consummation, for it is based on God's promise of ongoing renewal and transformation.

In the New Testament, the Gospel of John maintains a delicate eschatological balance between "the already and the not yet." Passages such as John 3:17–21, 31–36, and 6:47 exemplify realized eschatology. The very presence of Jesus in the world confronts the world with a decision, to believe or not to believe, and making that decision is the moment of judgment. John 3:18 explains that this judgment is underway in the present, initiated by Jesus' coming into the world (see 3:36). If one's life is characterized by transformative belief, so that one's deeds are "done in God" (John 3:21), then one *already* has eternal life (3:36); if one does not believe, one is *already* condemned. John's Gospel does include traditional understandings of eschatology and the final judgment (5:28–29; 12:48), but judgment and

---

1. Fowler, *Stages of Faith*, 205.

eternal life as present realities are at the theological heart of the Fourth Gospel.

As John affirmed eternal life as already present for the followers of Jesus, he also believed in realized wrath, that God's wrath is already present for those who reject and disobey God. For John, there are always moral consequences to one's actions, both sooner and later.

"Eternal life," the term John uses instead of "the Kingdom of God," is not something believers possess only after death. It begins as soon as one places trust in Jesus as God's Son. Contemporary Christians have become so used to associating eternal life with going to heaven that the idea of realized eschatology, which views the future as somehow present now, seems perplexing.

The notion of "eternal life," like the "Kingdom of God," is paradoxical at its core. In the Synoptic Gospels, the paradoxical nature of the Kingdom is manifested in several ways: (a) it is present (Matt. 12:28; Luke 17:21), yet not fully present (Matt. 8:29; 13:30); (b) it is a gift (Matt. 25:34; Luke 12:32), yet it also involves human effort (Luke 12:31); (c) it is an internal reality (Luke 17:20–21), yet it has external implications for the world (Matt. 6:10).

Eternal life, like the Kingdom of God, is already present, yet not fully so. This becomes clearer when we understand that "eternal life" has as much to do with the quality and direction of life as with the length of one's existence. A better term might be "everlasting life," meaning a life that begins for believers in this lifetime but continues on forever.

We live in a time of deep division, in which mind is at odds with body, and spirituality with matter. We need a way out of the dualistic attitudes that permeate our thinking, permeable boundaries between polarities such as good and evil, God and Satan, light and darkness, spirit and flesh, eternal life and eternal death, belief and disbelief, truth and falsehood, heaven and hell, heaven and earth. Dualism claims independent reality for each polarity, whereas the truth is that the negative item in the pair derives somehow from its opposite. As cold is the absence of heat, so evil is the absence of good, and so forth.

As the book of Revelation makes clear, soft boundaries exist between spatial and temporal planes and even between good and evil. Evil contrasts with good, but evil is not of a fundamentally different order from good. Even God and Satan, the epitome of good and evil respectively, are not separated by hard, impervious boundaries, for in the Bible the "demonic" plane derives from the heavenly, divine plane. While boundaries do exist between heaven and earth, future and present, deity and humanity, and good and evil, there is dynamism to boundaries. Boundaries do not fix limits beyond which it is impossible to pass. Rather they locate the place where transformations occur, allowing a flow across planes, eras, social categories, and moral values.

In the Bible, "heaven" is the starting point for all revelation. We should not, however, restrict "heaven" to the spiritual dimension of reality, for it represents more than that. In the book of Revelation, what John sees in heaven is not simply divine perspective. "Heaven" represents what is right and good and proper. When Jesus tells his followers to pray, "Your kingdom come . . . on earth as it is in heaven" (Matt. 6:10), he understands "heaven" not as a future destination for humans but as God's dimension of everyday reality. Heaven is in charge; heaven takes the lead; heaven represents what ought to be happening on earth now.

As we stressed earlier, to live with agape love now is to live out of the resources of the future, and when Christians live that way, they demonstrate not only the reality of eternal life, but the fact that it is available in the present. No one understood that better than Elizabeth Barrett Browning, who penned these memorable words:

> Earth's crammed with heaven,
> And every common bush afire with God;
> And he who sees it takes off his shoes—
> The rest sit round it and pluck blackberries.[2]

No one can live a good life alone, and no one can be moral in isolation. Learning and sustaining the virtues that transform a person who has the gifts of faith, hope, and love into a person with a full moral life require self-knowledge and self-disciple. The tasks are sometimes lonely, but they are not accomplished alone. We live our faith in a community with others, both in the community of faith that is the church and in the wider civic community. One of the most persistent questions of our time is whether these communities in which we live are the sorts of places that can support us in the effort to live a good life.

Can our churches teach us virtue? What should we make of the tensions, conflicts, and divisions among Christians that often seem to bring out the worst in them, rather than enable them to live at their best? Can we expect assistance in living virtuously from the businesses, schools, and

---

2. *Aurora Leigh*, Book VII, Line 820.

governments around us, or must we actively resist the values they teach in order to live a good life?

One thing is certain; the biblical emphasis on renewal is always "now": "*Now* is the acceptable time; now is the day of salvation" (2 Cor. 6:2), and "*Today*, if you hear his voice, do not harden your hearts" (Heb. 4:7). Those who expect apocalyptic solutions, whether through divine judgment at the end of history or via Christ's return, may wait indefinitely. If renewal is to occur, it must occur now.

Our task in the present, according to Jesus, is to ask, search, and knock: "Ask, and it will be given you; search, and you will find; knock, and the door will be opened for you. For everyone who asks receives, and everyone who searches find, and for everyone who knocks, the door will be opened" (Matt. 7:7–8). The emphasis here is active and present: these are things we need to be doing now. And if we strive first for the Kingdom of God and its righteousness, all good things will be given to us as well (Matt. 6:33).

As Paul indicates, God is a promissory God, fulfilling all promises in Christ (2 Cor. 1:20) and through the Holy Spirit, given as a guarantee of divine faithfulness (2 Cor. 5:5). God renews both cosmos and humanity by the Spirit, indwelling believers, inspiring their mission, and dispensing gifts freely by grace. And the message of Scripture is clear: this God loves us unconditionally.

To take eschatology seriously is to see that the hoped-for present comes to us out of the future. Receiving the present from God's future frees us from the shackles of the past. Seen in the light of biblical hope, the human vocation is to live in anticipation of the coming rule of God, leaning into God's promised future for us and for all being. To live this way is to be part of the reconciling, redeeming, and restoring work that goes on wherever the Kingdom of God is breaking in. Using Fowler's imagery, bearers of Stage 6 faith, whether they stand in Christian, Jewish, Muslim, or other faith traditions, embody radically this "leaning into" God's future for all being.[3]

According to the Bible, there is a moral force in the universe. Ultimately injustice will be defeated. As biblical prophets indicate, one cannot get away with injustice. God listens to the voice of the weak and the marginalized, and no individual, institution, or society that supports oppression is safe, whether secular or religious. As prophets know, challenging injustice produces hope, particularly hope for change on this earth. In that

---

3. Fowler, *Stages of Faith*, 210–11.

spirit, listen anew to the words Jesus taught his disciples to pray: "Your kingdom come, Your will be done, *on earth* as it is in heaven" (Matt. 6:10).

As we have seen, hope rooted in promise is related to change, not only for individuals but also for society. John of Patmos, visualizing a "new heaven and a new earth" (Rev. 21:1), quotes God as saying: "See, I am making all things new" (Rev. 21:5). When Jesus speaks of faith moving mountains (Mark 11:23), such mountains surely include problems that plague us today, evils such as racism, sexism, terrorism, militarism, jingoism, materialism, xenophobia, pollution, poverty, domestic violence, and addictive behavior.

As we sing in church: "Let there be peace on earth, and let it begin with me." When will this change happen? If it doesn't begin now, with us, it may not happen at all. What scourge will your faith help eliminate from our planet?

Christians, empowered by God's Spirit, are to live positively, as Jesus did, out of the resources of the Kingdom, rather than negatively, out of the resources of the moment. As citizens of God's Kingdom, Christians are to live as the salt of the earth and the light of the world (Matt. 5:13–16), rather than suspiciously, fearfully, and impotently.

If faith, hope, and love exist, as we have described them, basic to morality yet beyond human invention, then I submit they come as gifts from a benevolent deity. If God is as we have described—Lover, Giver, and Creator—then we live in a loving, moral universe, with grace as its cornerstone. Our responsibility, then, is to live graciously on planet earth, empowered by the resources of God, whose image we bear.

Summary

According to the Gospels, Jesus began his ministry by announcing that the time had come for God to begin God's reign on earth. The Good News of the gospel was not that God's Kingdom was about to be realized on earth, but rather that the Kingdom had actually arrived, and that its power was already present. Indeed, eternal life, the term John's Gospel uses instead of "the Kingdom of God," is already present, though not fully so. When Jesus speaks of faith moving mountains, such mountains include the problems that plague us today. Christian hope is not "pie in the sky by and by," but radical power to tackle head-on today's problems and to defeat them. To live with agape love now is to live out of the resources of the future, and

Realized Eschatology

when Christians live like that, they demonstrate not only the reality of eternal life, but the fact that it is available in the present.

For Discussion and Reflection

1. Do you agree that too many Christians seek Christ's return (known popularly as "the rapture" of believers to heaven) as the solution to the world's problems? Does Paul's advice to believers in his day "living in idleness" (that is, sitting and waiting for Christ's return; see 2 Thess. 3:6–15) apply to the current mindset of those who wait for "the rapture" as a solution to the world's evil?
2. In a sentence or two define what is meant by "the Kingdom of God."
3. Evaluate the perspective called "realized eschatology," including the merits and disadvantages of holding such a view.
4. In the epilogue, the author utilizes John's Gospel in support of "realized eschatology." Should John's perspective be viewed as a peculiarity of that gospel, or should John's emphasis on "the already" nature of the Kingdom be determinative for Christian thinking and living?
5. Should we think of "heaven" primarily as a place of future reward or primarily as "God's dimension of everyday reality," as the text suggests? What difference might these alternative ways of thinking about "heaven" have on our lifestyle?
6. In your estimation, what does Elizabeth Barrett Browning mean in her poem when she writes: "he who sees it takes off his shoes"? What is she suggesting by the words, "The rest sit round it and pluck blackberries"?
7. When Jesus spoke of faith moving mountains (Mark 11:23), which social "mountain" will your faith help to eliminate from our planet?
8. If you were to live as the "salt" of the earth and as the "light" of the world, what changes in your life might these require?

Appendix A

Table of Interrelated Virtues

GRACE	LOVE	HOPE	FAITH
Prudence (Intellectual)	*Justice* (Volitional)	*Fortitude* (Emotional)	*Temperance* (Social)
Wisdom	Impartiality	Courage	Moderation
Mindfulness	Compassion	Diligence	Restraint
Practicality	Kindness	Honesty	Loyalty
Curiosity	Forgiveness	Optimism	Truthfulness
Reverence	Respectfulness	Self-Discipline	Reliability
Creativity	Integrity	Patience	Gratitude
Objectivity	Sincerity	Vitality	Modesty
Awe/Wonder	Generosity	Humor	Humility
Honesty	Cooperation	Excellence	Frugality
Reflection	Tolerance	Trust	Contentment

    The preceding table of virtues, with their correspondences, is suggestive. Concepts such as grace, love, hope, and faith transcends the rational, the unconscious, the voluntary, and the emotional structures of the person while including all of them at the same time. The same can be said for the cardinal virtues and their sub-categories. Moderation, for example, is often associated with temperance, but it plays a useful role as well in prudence, justice, and fortitude.

Appendix B

The Seven Virtues: A Brief Look

A LIST OF THE seven heavenly virtues, to oppose the seven deadly sins, first appeared in an epic poem entitled *Psychomachia or Battle/Contest of the Soul*. Written by Aurelius Clemens Prudentius, a Christian governor who died around AD 410, this work entails the battle between good virtues and evil vices. The enormous popularity of this work in the Middle Ages helped to spread the concept of holy virtue throughout Europe.

As we grow in faith, hope, love, and grace, it will be helpful to explore more deeply the meaning of the seven virtues, particularly if practicing them helps us overcome weakness and temptation. Below are some qualities traditionally associated with the seven virtues:

- *Chastity* (vice: *lust*)—purity of thought; moral wholeness; discretion of sexual conduct; good health and hygiene; refraining from intoxicants; honesty with oneself, family, friends, and all others.

- *Abstinence* (vice: *gluttony*)—restraint, temperance, justice; mindfulness of others; practicing self-control and deferred gratification; prudence to judge the appropriateness of actions at a given time; appropriate moderation between self-interest and public interest, mindful of the rights and needs of others.

- *Liberality* (vice: *greed*)—self-sacrificial lifestyle; charity; generosity; agape love; unlimited lovingkindness toward all people.

The Seven Virtues: A Brief Look

- *Diligence* (vice: *sloth*)—a healthy work ethic; wise use of time; integrity at all times, especially when no one is watching; steadfastness in belief; fortitude; endurance with dignity; the capacity to not be a quitter.
- *Patience* (vice: *anger*)—endurance through moderation; resolving conflict and injustice peacefully; not resorting to violence; showing mercy to wrongdoers.
- *Kindness* (vice: *envy*)—compassion; empathy and trust of others without resentment; friendship for its own sake; inspiring others with a cheerful demeanor and a positive outlook.
- *Humility* (vice: *pride*)—(to be humble does not mean to think less of oneself, but to think of oneself less); charity toward those with whom you disagree; giving credit where credit is due; the courage of heart necessary to undertake tasks that are tedious or unglamorous; respect for public servants, people in authority, and toward one's elders; keeping one's promises as far as possible.

Appendix C

Love Never Fails: A Sermon

In 1935, at the height of the Depression, my parents became married and three weeks later they left every security—their family, friends, jobs, most of their meager belongings, and even their country—for the adventure of a lifetime as missionaries in Costa Rica, then a world far away. There they began a new vocation, immersing themselves in a new culture, eating different food, observing different traditions, learning a different language, and even worshipping in a different manner.

They were guided by three principles, simple notions yet so powerful they can transform anyone's life, enabling ordinary people to live extraordinary lives. The three principles, discussed in 1 Corinthians 13, one of the best loved chapters in the Bible, are well-known today: faith, hope, and love.

Background to 1 Corinthians 13

1 Corinthians 13 is known as the love chapter or the Hymn of Love[1]. Many people know it as a detached poem, often read at weddings. Some scholars read this passage as a free literary unit, arguing that this literary gem is so well composed and of such high quality that it might well have been composed separately and only later inserted at this point. I prefer a different understanding of the chapter and its purpose, understanding its meaning and message in literary context.

---

1. The text of 1 Corinthians 13 is recorded on the epigraph page at the front of this book.

Love Never Fails: A Sermon

This passage is best understood when it is viewed as part of a three-act play involving the community of believers at Corinth, or better yet, as a symphony in three movements. Chapter 12 is the opening movement, with an introduction (verses 1–11) concerning the variety of gifts given to Christians and how these gifts are to be used for the common good. The movement's main theme or central tune is then stated in verses 12–13 (the Church—Christ's body—is one unity, though it has many parts). The theme is then explored from several angles (verses 14–26 = the development section), before the recapitulation or restatement of the theme in verses 27–31.

Chapter 13—our passage—can best be understood as a second movement, an adagio, if you will, a lyrical yet powerful section of the symphony. Paul knew that his listener-readers needed to pause in their thinking about his message, to move into a different key and rhythm, and so he challenges them to focus on the highest virtue, the greatest quality, the supreme way of life. What he provides in chapter 13 is a living illustration, a description of the most sublime way to live, a unique picture of Jesus and of the most Christ-like characteristic one can imagine: selfless agape love.

Completing our analogy of a symphony, chapter 14, delivers the extensive third movement, in which Paul takes the theory laid out in chapter 12, depicted vividly in chapter 13, and gives practical application to specific problems in the Corinthian church.

When we examine this great love chapter in its literary and historical context, we find ourselves overwhelmed by a startling realization: What inspired this great poem was neither an ideal congregation nor a perfect pastoral setting. Rather it was a struggling, conflicted congregation in the notoriously immoral port city of Corinth.

Here is one modern person's description of Corinth in Paul's day: "Corinth was the Vanity Fair of ancient Greece: a sailor's favorite port, a prodigal's paradise, a policeman's nightmare, and a preacher's graveyard." The point is that Paul saved his most inspiring, most hopeful, most enduring message for his most problematic congregation, located in one of the most godless, pagan settings of his day.

Remarkably, the message of 1 Corinthians 13 is just as applicable today, to Christian denominations polarized over critical issues such as the Lordship of Christ, the authority of Scripture, and the application of biblical standards to a myriad of social and personal issues emanating from a secular worldview and a postmodern culture.

1 Corinthians 13:13 introduces three qualities so eternal and enduring that theologians have grouped them together under the category of "supernatural virtues." Thomas Aquinas, the great medieval theologian, contrasted these with the four cardinal or natural virtues: prudence, justice, fortitude, and temperance. These four, he argued, God expects us to attain. But the "supernatural virtues" come from God, and they can be achieved only with divine assistance. Hence throughout history faith, hope, and love have been called "theological graces," as opposed to other virtues, which are also called "gifts," and well they are.

Analysis of the Supernatural Virtues

Let us examine faith and hope first, before we consider the third grace, and why love is said to be greater than faith and hope.

FAITH—In Hebrews 11:1 we find a classic definition of faith: "Now faith is the assurance of things hoped for, the conviction of things not see." As this statement makes clear, faith is based on "assurance," meaning divine promise, but faith is also based on "conviction," translated in some Bibles as "evidence" (KJV; NAB), meaning that faith should be viewed as reliable and foundational for life. In the Bible, faith is the trustful acceptance of (a) God's promises, particularly bless all the peoples and nations of the world. But faith is also (b) a trust in God's faithfulness to the promise, that is, in God's ability to deliver Good News to everyone, something God accomplished through Jesus Christ and his followers, and that includes us. Faith comes first in this trilogy of graces. Without Faith we cannot have Hope, and without Hope we cannot have true, agape Love.

When my parents left for a foreign land in 1935, they went by faith. They staked their lives on the promises of Scripture and on the faithfulness of God. As career missionaries, first in the idyllic country of Costa Rica, then in turbulent Colombia, they trusted God implicitly. They did not know what lay ahead—the glorious highs and the gut-wrenching lows—but they trusted God implicitly. And they were not disappointed.

HOPE—John Calvin called hope "perseverance in faith," meaning never giving up on God's faithfulness or compromising reliance on God's promises. Faith and hope are inseparable because hope is faith taken to the next level. Believers whose lives and attitudes are characterized by faith and hope might be labelled "optimists" by non-believers, simply because they seem to be positive and upbeat, but most often they are viewed as naïve or fools, because they believe in something invisible or hope for something unrealistic.

However, faith and hope are not limited to happy days or to good times. College students get nervous when I tell them that the best way to become mature people of faith is to face their deepest fears as well as the greatest problems of their lifetime, including global warming; pandemics; terrorism; overpopulation; urban unrest; global hunger; religious wars; substance abuse and other addictions; erosion of religious and personal values, economic woes; air and water pollution; scarcity of resources; denominational schisms; and so forth. When we ponder these threats, we panic.

But I remember when traumatic, life-changing calamities struck my parents, how my father lost an eye in a sledding accident when he was ten years of age, or how my mother contracted cancer at the age of forty-eight, while in the prime of her life, at a time when she was fully engaged in a care-giving ministry for the God she loved and served. And it was breast cancer, quite possibly a woman's worst fear. A mastectomy was performed, and after several months of improving health, my mother discovered another lump forming in her other breast. Was this spreading of cancer an indication that her ministry, perhaps even her life, was at an end, or was this experience a "wound of love," like the limp that the Old Testament patriarch Jacob received when he wrestled with God, when he received a new name (Israel) and a renewed promise for himself and his posterity?

This event came at a time when my parents were about to experience a deepening of their faith and an enlarging of their ministry. My mother would go on to live forty additional years as a cancer survivor. My father became ordained to the gospel ministry in 1966, two years before his retirement, and he spent the next twenty-five years teaching himself Greek and Hebrew, eventually reading the entire Bible in the original languages, something few Seminary graduates or Bible scholars have ever accomplished. And he did this only with the use of one eye.

As a young adult, discouraged and downhearted, I confronted my parents with a litany of doomsday scenarios. Without a moment's hesitation, my mother responded out of the reservoir of hope that had fueled her faith during times when her life was at risk, particularly as a missionary in Colombia—the Syria and Iraq of its day in the sense of deep sectarian violence and conflict and the place that inspired Fidel Castro to become a militant Marxist. My mother's response on that day when I was confronting my fears was hopeful and unwavering: "The best is yet to come." She knew, quoting Corrie ten Boom, the Dutch Christian lady who survived the concentration camps where she was sent for harboring Jews during World War II, that "There is no pit so deep that God's love is not deeper still."

My wife, Susan, a pastoral counselor, asks her clients to address the worst consequence that can result from the situation they are facing, for she has learned from experience that when persons are willing to confront their deepest fear, this becomes the first step to victory. Faith and hope are inseparable, but they should not be confused with mere wish-fulfillment. They are most powerful when they are related to the real world, to such things as crosses and cancers.

LOVE—When we examine the third grace, love, we wonder why Paul says in I Cor. 13:8 that "love never fails," or, stated more literally, why love "never collapses."

To answer that question we need to distinguish between two related words in Greek: (1) *philia* (affection), which is a genuine love and compassion for others, but generally refers to "love of the deserving," and (2) *agape*, Paul's word here, which means "love of the undeserving." The classic expression of agape is Romans 5:8: "But God shows his love for us in that while we were yet sinners Christ died for us." It is agape, God's love, that never fails, for human love, even at its best, regularly fails us, often when we need it most.

We come to the question that has been dogging us for some time: Why is love said to be greater than faith and hope? Let me suggest two answers. First, of these three virtues, only agape endures, not only because it comes from God, but because love is an extension of God's eternal nature. Furthermore, agape is greater than faith and hope because these are designated for the present life, whereas agape is the way of life in the new world to come. Therefore, to love with agape love now is to live life out of the resources of the future, and when Christians live life that way, they demonstrate not only the reality of eternal life, but the fact that it is available in the present and not just as a future hope. They know, as Elizabeth Barrett Browning did, that "Earth's crammed with heaven, And every common bush afire with God."

The King James Version translation of agape by "charity" is unfortunate, for in today's culture the term is used mostly with administering relief to people in need. Agape is more than mere sentiment and clearly transcends human affection. Agape is an attitude of the heart, of the mind, and of the will; agape energizes and activates the whole of one's personality. Agape is the highest form of knowing, the highest form of being, and the highest form of living. Such love is only possible for those who live in the power of the indwelling Christ. Oh to be driven by such a singular purpose! Agape is greater than all of the spiritual gifts put together. Without agape, spiritual gifts are empty and vain. Earnestly desire the spiritual gifts, Paul exhorts in 1 Corinthians 14:1, but make agape your aim.

Conclusion

An excellent illustration of agape comes from the life of Mother Teresa, who devoted her life to serving the untouchables of Calcutta. In 1988 I heard her speak to an audience gathered for the General Assembly of the Presbyterian Church in St. Louis. As she entered the room all rose to their feet in admiration. A reporter once asked her the secret of her remarkable ministry: "How have you accomplished this?" Mother Teresa responded by pointing upward and stating simply, "God has done it all. I have done nothing."

So there you have it, three principles that, taken together, are guaranteed to transform your life. We start with faith. Faith leads to Hope, and out of Hope comes Love—love of the undeserving. And that Love Never Fails. Amen.

Bibliography

Armstrong, Karen. *The Case for God*. New York: Anchor, 2010.
Benedict XVI, Pope. *Spe Salvi*. Rome: Libreria Editrice Vaticana, 2007. No pages. Online: w2.vatican.va/content/benedict-xvi/en/encyclicals/documents/hf_ben-xvi_enc_20071130_spe-salvi.html.
Borg, Marcus. *The Heart of Christianity*. New York: HarperSanFrancisco, 2004.
Bourgeault, Cynthia. *The Holy Trinity and the Law of Three*. Boston, Shambhala, 2013.
Christian, William A. *Meaning and Truth in Religion*. Princeton, NJ: Princeton University Press, 1964.
Daniels, David N. and Virginia A. Price. *The Essential Enneagram*. New York: HarperOne, 2009.
Eliade, Mircea. *The Sacred and the Profane: The Nature of Religion*. Orlando, FL: Harcourt Brace Jovanovich, 1987.
Esposito, John Esposito, et al. *World Religions Today*. New York: Oxford University Press, 2001.
Fowler, James W. *Stages of Faith*. New York: Harper & Row, 1981.
Fox, Matthew. *Creation Spirituality*. New York: HarperSanFrancisco, 1991.
———. *Original Blessing*. Santa Fe, NM: Bear & Co., 1983.
Haught, John. *Deeper Than Darwin: The Prospect for Religion in an Age of Evolution*. Boulder, CO: Westview, 2003.
———. *The Promise of Nature*. Mahwah, NJ: Paulist, 1993.
———. *Responses to 101 Questions on God and Evolution*. Mahwah, NJ: Paulist, 2001.
———. *Science and Religion: From Conflict to Conversation*. Mahway, NJ: Paulist, 1995.
Kuhn, Thomas. *The Structure of Scientific Revolutions*. Chicago: The University of Chicago Press, 1970.
Lesser, Elizabeth. *The Seeker's Guide: Making Your Life a Spiritual Adventure*. New York: Villard, 2000.
Lewis, C. S. *The Abolition of Man*. New York: Macmillan, 1947.
———. *The Four Loves*. New York: Harcourt Brace, 1960.
———. *The Great Divorce*. New York: HarperOne, 2015 (1945).
———. *Mere Christianity*. New York: Collier, 1952.
———. *Surprised by Joy*. New York: Harcourt, Brace, Jovanovich, 1966.
———. "The Weight of Glory," 1–9. Online: www.verber.com/mark/xian/weight-of-glory.pdf.
Lovin, Robin W. *Christian Ethics: An Essential Guide*. Nashville, TN: Abingdon, 2000.

Bibliography

McGrath, Alister E. *Christian Theology: An Introduction.* 5th. ed. Malden: MA, 2011.
Moltmann, Jürgen. *Theology of Hope.* New York: Harper & Row, 1967.
Moore, James. *Gurdjieff: The Anatomy of a Myth.* Rockport, MA: Element, 1991.
Peck, M. Scott. *The Different Drum.* New York: Simon & Schuster, 1987.
Polkinghorne, John. *Belief in God in an Age of Science.* New Haven, CT: Yale University Press, 1998.
———. *One World: The Interaction of Science and Theology.* Princeton, NJ: Princeton University Press, 1987.
———. *Quarks, Chaos and Christianity: Questions to Science and Religion.* New York: Crossroad, 1998.
Riso, Don Richard and Russ Hudson. *Personality Types: Using the Enneagram for Self-Discovery.* Rev. ed. New York: Houghton Mifflin, 1996.
———. *The Wisdom of the Enneagram.* New York: Bantam, 1999.
Rohr, Richard, and Andreas Ebert. *The Enneagram: A Christian Perspective.* Rev. ed. New York: Crossroad, 2001.
Smith, Huston. *Forgotten Truth: The Common Vision of the World's Religions.* New York: HarperSanFrancisco, 1976.
Smith, Wilfred Cantwell. *Belief and History.* Charlottsville, VA: University Press of Virginia, 1977.
———. *Faith and Belief.* Princeton, NJ: Princeton University Press, 1979.
———. *The Meaning and End of Religion.* New York: Macmillan, 1963.
Streng, Fred, et al. *Ways of Being Religious.* Englewood Cliffs, NJ: Prentice-Hall, 1973.
Tillich, Paul. *Dynamics of Faith.* New York: Harper & Row, 1957.
Vande Kappelle, Robert. *Beyond Belief.* Eugene, OR: Wipf & Stock, 2012.
Wright, N. T. *Paul for Everyone: 1 Corinthians.* Louisville, KY: Westminster John Knox, 2004.
Young, William A. *The World's Religions; Worldviews and Contemporary Issues.* Upper Saddle River, NJ: Prentice-Hall, 2010.

Subject/Name Index

Abraham, 29–30, 49, 85, 86, 88
abstinence, 64, 89, 115, 134
agape. *See* love, agape
anger, 114, 115, 135
Anselm of Canterbury, 90
anthropology, anthropologist, 19–20
    theistic, 20
Apostles Creed, 31
Aquinas, Thomas, 8, 60, 61, 63, 64, 65,
    68, 74, 106, 107, 138
arête, 61
Aristotle (philosopher), 12–13, 60, 61,
    63, 107
Armstrong, Karen, ix, 72n3
Augustine, Augustinian, 4, 26, 37, 74,
    94–95, 107
avarice, 115, 116
    See also greed

Bacharach, Burt, 94
Bahai, 52
Basic Desire. *See* Enneagram, Basic
    Desire
Basic Fear. *See* Enneagram, Basic Fear
Beatitudes, 50
belief(s), believe, 71–73, 77
    faith and, 72–74
Benedict XVI, Pope, 82
binary perspective. *See* dualistic
    thought
body, human, 14, 15, 16–17
Boff, Leonardo, 44
Borg, Marcus, ix, 73n4
boson (Higgs), 14

Bourgeault, Cynthia, 9n9
Boy Scouts, 7–8
Brahman, 54, 107
Browning, Elizabeth Barrett, 128, 140
Buddha, 49
Buddhism, 50, 52
    Eightfold Path of, 50, 52

Calvin, John, 88, 138
Campbell, Joseph, 26
Castro, Fidel, 139
charity, 97, 134, 135 140
chastity, 115, 134
Christian, William A., 28
Christianity, 53, 56
    and hope, 82–83, 88, 91
    essential beliefs of, 77
Cicero (Roman orator), 26, 60
community, principle of, 6
compassion, 43–44
Confucianism, 53
cosmology, cosmologies, 11, 19–20
    and morality, 21
    anthropological, 19–20
    definition of, 19
    models of, 12
    scientific, 13, 19–20
cosmos
    as story, 35
    origin of, 1, 20, 35
    purpose of, 35–40
courage. *See* fortitude
creation spirituality, 7n7, 42–44

Subject/Name Index

Daniels, David N., 110n4
Daoism (Taoism), 53
  See also Tao (Dao)
Darwin, Charles, 37
David, Hal, 93
detachment, 116
diligence, 134
Dirac, Paul, 14
Dodd, C. H., 125
doubt(s). See faith, and doubt
dualistic (binary) thought, 9n9, 23–24, 42, 127
Dyson, Freeman, 40

Ebert, Andreas, 110n4
Einstein, Albert, 11, 13
election, 29–30
Eliade, Mircea, 24
Enneagram, 110–22, 123
  and transformational growth, 112–13, 114–15, 118–21, 122
  Basic Desire, 118–19
  Basic Fear, 118
  defense of, 113–14, 121–22
  Direction of Disintegration, 119–20
  Direction of Integration, 120–21
  Law of Seven, 112
  Law of Three, 112–13
  model of, 111
  origins of, 112–13
  personality types in, 112, 115–18
entropy, 34, 36
envy, 114, 115, 116, 135
Erikson, Erik, 108
eschatology, 82–83, 124, 129
  See also realized eschatology
Esposito, John, 24–25
eternal life, 127, 131
ethics
  Christian, 5
Evagrius of Pontus (monk), 112
evil, 40, 42
evolution, biological, 36–40
Exodus, 29

faith, 70–78, 130, 138
  and belief. See belief, faith and
  and doubt, 74, 77, 78
  and hope, 81–82, 84, 90–91, 104–5
  biblical understanding of, 71–72
  primary meanings, 73–78
  stages of, 108–10
fear, 117
fortitude, 62, 64, 107, 117, 133, 138
Fourth Way, 112
Fowler, James, 108–9, 123, 129
Fox, Matthew, 7n7, 42–44
Francis of Assisi (monk), 122
freedom, 76

Gandhi, M. K. (Mahatma), 62n2
Gestalt Pastoral Care, 122
Girl Scouts, 7–8
gluttony, 115, 117, 134
goals, 5, 6
God, 3n3, 44, 76, 104, 105, 130
  and energy, 1–2
  and moral virtues, 8, 68
  and renewal, 88, 99, 129
  as Creator, 4–5, 42, 43, 98, 104
  as gracious, 104, 105
  as Life, 3
  as love, 95–97
  as personal, 1
  as Spirit, 1, 18–19, 37
  faithfulness of, 75, 86, 129, 138
  love of, 4, 95–97, 99–100, 104, 107, 108, 129, 140, 141
  particle. See boson
  trust in, 84, 86
Golden Mean (Doctrine of the Mean), 61–62, 65
Golden Rule, 50
Gould, Stephen Jay, 34
grace, 98, 103, 104–5, 106, 122, 129
  human development and 107–8, 110, 133
Great Commandment, the, 26, 75, 96
greed, 115, 116, 134
Gurdjieff, G., I., 112–13, 121
  personality types, 112–13

happiness, 3
Haught, John, 36, 39n4, 41
heaven, 89, 127, 128
Heraclitus (philosopher), 12

Subject/Name Index

Hinduism, 54, 60
Holy Spirit, 85, 104, 129, 130
   and love, 95, 96
   fruit of the, 76
hope, 80–91, 133, 138–40
   biblical understanding of, 83–85
   faith and, 81–82, 90, 104
   for the cosmos, 36–38, 42
   primary meanings of, 86–88, 90–91
Hudson, Russ, 110n4, 122
humility, 115, 135

Ichazo, Oscar, 113
intelligence, forms of, 70
Islam, 54
   Five Pillars in, 50, 54

Jagger, Mick, 88
Jainism, 54
Jeans, James, 34
Jesus Christ, 11–12, 49, 71, 88, 104, 129
   and discipleship, 71
   and Kingdom of God, 125–27, 129
   and love, 96–97
   and the good life, 4
   belief in, 71–72
   hope in, 83
John, Gospel of, 60–61
   and realized eschatology, 126–27
Judaism, 55, 87
justice, 63–64, 107, 117, 133, 138

kindness, 115, 135
Kingdom of God, 125–27, 129, 130
knowing, ways of, 70
Kohlberg, Lawrence, 108
Kuhn, Thomas, 44

Lactantius (early Christian author), 26
Law of Seven, 112
Law of Three, 112–13
Lesser, Elizabeth, 16
Lewis, C. S., ix, 60, 88–90
   and discipleship, 89–90
   and heaven, 89
   and longing, 88–89
   and love, 97–100
life, 37

goodness of, 2, 3–4
   purpose of, 3
Lord's Prayer, 125, 126, 130
love, 93–101, 133
   agape, 97, 98–101, 140–41
   analogy of, 95
   biblical understanding of, 95–97
   for God, 99
   primary meanings of, 97–98, 140–41
Lovin, Robin, ix, 4–5, 62n4, 80n1, 93n1, 104n1
lust, 115, 117, 134

McGrath, Alistair, 31
metaphysics, 9n9, 16
mind, human, 15–17
mission statement, 5, 7
moderation, 133
Muhammad, 49
Moltmann, Jürgen, 82

Naranjo, Claudio, 113
natural law, 60–61
nature
   abundance of, 2
   and design, 37–38
   and promise, 35–41
   as sacrament, 41–42
   goodness of, 2
Norberg, Tilda, 122

Pacwa, Mitch, S. J., 113
Parmenides (philosopher), 12
particle colliders, 13
Pascal, Blaise, 71
patience, 115, 135
Paul (apostle), 68–69 76, 129
   and cosmic hope, 36, 88
   and grace, 105
   and hope, 84–85
   and love, 97, 98, 99, 100, 140–41
   and natural law, 60
   and religious pluralism, 56
   and theological virtues, 8
Peck, M. Scott, 108, 110
personality types. *See* Enneagram, personality types
Piaget, Jean, 108

Subject/Name Index

Plato (philosopher), 12, 107, 112
Polkinghorne, John, 70
Price, Virginia A, 110n4
pride, 72, 115, 116, 135
process theology, 39
    and God, 39
promise, cosmic, 35–41
    hope as, 86–88, 130
prudence, 62–63, 107, 115, 133, 138
Prudentius, Aurelius Clemens, 134
Pythagoras (philosopher), 112

reality
    levels of, 14–16
    sacramental nature of, 41–42
    three views of, 76–77
realized eschatology, 89n10, 124–31
reason (intellect), 68–69, 70, 77, 78
religion
    as noun or as adjective, 24–25
    definition of, 27–29
    etymology of, 26–27
    role of, 23, 28–29, 47–56
resentment, 114
Revelation, book of, 127, 130
Riso, Don R., 110n4, 122
rita, 60
Rohr, Richard, 110n4
rules, 59, 61

sacrament, 41
Sagan, Carl, 34
salvation, 29–32
science
    and religion, 1–2
    and teleology, 34, 35–37
    paradigms shifts in, 44
self
    levels of, 14–17
self-control, 116
shame, 114
Shinto, 55
Sikhism, 55
sin(s), 28, 31, 40–41
    original, 42
    seven, 115

See also evil
sloth, 115, 118, 134
Smart, Ninian, 48
Smith, Huston, ix, 14–19
    reality and the self, 14–17
    spiritual personality types, 18–19
Smith, Wilfred Cantwell, 72n3
Spirit. *See* Holy Spirit
spirituality, ix, 16, 17, 42, 44, 80, 99, 108
    Christian, 93, 99
stewardship, principle of, 6
Streng, Fred, 28

Tao (Dao), 53, 60, 107
temperance, 64–65, 107, 117, 133, 138
ten Boom, Corrie, 140
Teresa, Mother, 100, 141
ternary perspective, 9n9, 112
Tillich, Paul, 28
Tolkien, J. R. R., 90
Torah, 60
Trinity, Holy, 9n9, 94–95
trust, 74–75, 78
    hope and, 86
truth
    literal, 49
    mythological, 49
truthfulness, 116

vanity, 116
vices, 134–35
    in Enneagram, 115–18
virtues, 61–62
    cardinal (natural), 8, 59–66
    in Enneagram, 115–18
    seven, 8, 115, 134–35
    theological (supernatural), 8–9, 67–101, 138–41

Warwick, Dionne, 93
Whitehead, Alfred North, 39
Wilson, E. O., 34
Wright, N. T., 97

Young, William A., 28

www.ingramcontent.com/pod-product-compliance
Lightning Source LLC
Chambersburg PA
CBHW071508150426
43191CB00009B/1449